The Woman's Secret

of a

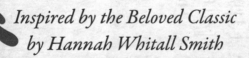

Happy Life

*Inspired by the Beloved Classic
by Hannah Whitall Smith*

Donna K. Maltese

SHILOH RUN PRESS

Especially for

_____

From

_____

Date

_____

CONTENTS

God's power is working in us. . . .
Our hearts ache,
but we always have joy.
We are poor,
but we give spiritual riches to others.
We own nothing,
and yet we have everything.

2 Corinthians 6:7, 10 nlt

Introduction

Joy is more than a feeling; it is a deep peace,
blended together with a solid hope
that God has not left us. Joy is a delight in
knowing there will be a better day.
Can we have joy as our companion even
when the road gets bumpy? Absolutely.
KAROL LADD, *THE POWER OF A POSITIVE WOMAN*

Who is responsible for realizing happiness in your life? You and you alone.

The Bible tells us that there are two kinds of happiness. The first is contingent upon what is happening around us, what our circumstances are. In other words, if things in our earthly existence are going well, we are happy.

But there is an even deeper happiness for Christians—one not contingent on our earthly situation. Instead it is based on a calm assurance that *in spite of* what is happening around us, we are trusting in Jesus, certain that the Holy Spirit is with us and that God will work all things out for our good. It's about rising above the trials and tribulations of this life to find that unspeakable happiness, that calmness, that sweet assurance in knowing that through flood and fire, the Lord's light is upon us, shining through us, exuding a peace that others are attracted to and yearn to possess.

You have the choice to be joyful or fearful, to hand your burdens over to Jesus or keep them firmly in your white-knuckled grip, to feel a growing hopelessness and desperation or feed a deep sense of peace. It is a choice you make each and every moment of every day, regardless of your circumstances.

This does not mean plastering a fake smile on your face but rather learning to be *joy*ful instead of *woe*ful. Unlike the "worldlings" who allow their emotions to rise and fall like the stock market, we Christians are to be abiding in the love and joy of Christ. If we are women of the Way (the term once used to describe Christians [see Acts 9:2; 19:9, 23; 22:4; 24:14, 22], based on Jesus' description of Himself in John 14:6), that deep, abiding joy is ours for the taking. But society can influence us to attempt to become everything it thinks we should be—thin and beautiful, wonderful mothers, successful career women, chefs, and housemaids. In this strive for worldly perfection, we can lose sight of what's real—the happiness of abiding in the Lord, the power of the Word, and the inspiration of the Holy Spirit.

So let's settle down to the fact that we are women of the Way. We are tired of being ruled by the world and are ready to embark upon a joyful journey. This does not mean we will ignore the world's myriad woes, but we will no longer allow them to rule our state of mind or influence our sense of peace.

So take off your apron, close up your briefcase, ditch the diaper bag, slip off your work shoes, and settle into a comfortable chair. Ask God to turn your funeral dirge into a joyful hymn, to take away your suit of mourning and clothe you with joy (see Psalm 30:11). Open your heart and mind and allow *The Woman's Secret of a Happy Life* to help you in your quest for lasting and deep happiness.

*T*his book was inspired by and is based in part on a classic, *The Christian's Secret of a Happy Life*, by Hannah Whitall Smith.

> *Born into a strict Quaker home in Pennsylvania in 1832, Hannah Whitall suffered from deep spiritual doubts during her early years. Her inner struggle continued into her marriage to Robert Piersall Smith in 1851, but in 1858 the couple committed their lives to Christ and decided to leave the Quaker faith to join the Plymouth Brethren.*
>
> *A further spiritual experience in 1867 led Hannah and Robert to undertake a speaking tour on the higher Christian life in the United States and Europe. As Robert's health declined, the couple stayed in England and observed the 1874 founding of the Keswick Convention. It was at a Keswick conference in 1886 that Amy Carmichael would feel the call of God to the mission field.*
>
> *Hannah Whitall Smith penned* The Christian's Secret of a Happy Life *in 1875*

and wrote eighteen other books as well, including The Unselfishness of God and How I Discovered It *in 1903. She was active in the Women's Christian Temperance Union, supported women's suffrage and other issues of gender equality, and studied the various religious movements that blossomed in the late nineteenth century.*

Smith was stricken with arthritis for the last seven years of her life and was ultimately confined to a wheelchair, but she still entertained admirers of her writings. She died in 1911.

It is our hope that within the pages of *The Woman's Secret of a Happy Life*, you will find inspiration and guidance on the pathway to the joy of the Lord, tapping into Christ's amazing power and strength as you mount up with wings as eagles.

> *And these things write we unto you,*
> *that your joy may be full.*
> 1 JOHN 1:4 KJV

How to Use This Book

The Woman's Secret of a Happy Life can be used to find your way into the joy of the Lord each and every day. The three sections of the book cover exactly what the higher life is, the challenges along the way, and the results it brings. At the end of each chapter, you will find Path Markers relating to the material covered in that chapter. They include a key Bible *promise*, its *proof*, God's *provision* for its pursuit, and part of your *portrait*. Claim each promise, allowing the reality of its proof to sink deep. With God's provision, determine to pursue that chapter's aspect of your faith. Part of this life-changing pursuit of happiness involves shifting not only your view of God's work in your life but the view you have of yourself. So carefully examine your portrait—a statement derived from a Bible passage that tells you who you truly are in Christ—and commit to memory who you are in the eyes of God.

These Path Markers will be followed by seven Mind-Renewing Prayers, one for each day of the week (or longer if you'd like to linger in a chapter until you believe you have truly found renewal). This will give you a chance to apply what you've learned and retrain your mind to focus on Jesus and the abundant joy found in Him instead of on the world and its life-sapping woes. For God's Word tells us, "Be careful what you think, because your thoughts run your life" (Proverbs 4:23 NCV). In other words, our thoughts fuel our feelings, and our feelings orchestrate our actions.

As you pray, read the words of each Mind-Renewing Prayer aloud and add whatever the Spirit brings to your heart. Remember that communicating with God is a two-way street. In the midst of your prayers, take the time to be still and listen for His voice.

There is no magic formula to obtaining joy. It is embedding yourself in the Word and embedding the Word in yourself—mind, body, and soul. It's trusting the One who has only the best in mind for you—regardless of how things may look, feel, or seem. It's waiting on God with hope: "Let Your lovingkindness, O LORD, be upon us, according as we have hoped in You" (Psalm 33:22 NASB).

Take to heart every line of God's truth. Claim each as your very own. Believe that your life may be embellished by actualizing His truths into your experiences. Above all, be patient with yourself. It takes time to reconstruct and readjust your attitude to life, God, yourself, and your surroundings. But never give up. God has a wonderful plan for your life. He is not only abiding with you on your inward journey but will give you victory without.

Please don't rush this process. Allow the aspects of each chapter to sink into your soul. Only move on to the next topic when you feel the Spirit's nudging to take the next step.

We wait for the LORD.
He is our help and our shield.
In him our hearts find joy.
In his holy name we trust.
PSALM 33:20–21 GW

Pray:

*L*ord, we are women of the Way. As such, we know that we are not to be caught up in the cares of this world but instead filled with Your joy. Open our eyes and hearts to Your Word. Help us to discover Your beauty in the people and things surrounding us. Enlighten our minds and allow the joy we find to feed our spirits. Amen.

PART 1:

The Life

Chapter 1:
Is Our Joyful Deliverance Scriptural?

If we're willing to let truth speak louder than our feelings,
and long enough that our feelings finally agree,
we can be far more than okay.
We can be delivered to a place where the air is crisp,
the enemy whipped, and the view is magnificent.
BETH MOORE, *GET OUT OF THAT PIT*

....

When we first encountered Jesus, we were filled with excitement and energy, ready to take on the world. Having shed our "old woman," we knew that from then on life would be a glorious, joy-filled ride. We thought, *How cool is this! I've got the world at my feet. Nothing can stop me now! From here on in, life will be a bed of roses! Everything will be great, swell! With Jesus, I've got it made!*

But as the months and years passed, the mountains we felt empowered to move began to bury us. Instead of continually tapping into Christ's power, we felt tapped out. Instead of conquering sin, we bowed to its influence over and over again until guilt began to take hold. As repeat offenders, we doubted God's mercy and forgiveness. Filled with shame and discouragement, we distanced ourselves from the very source of light, love, peace, power, and joy that had rescued us. Like Eve in the garden, we hid from the very One who could—and already did—save us.

Although we are weary, sorrow laden, and worn, we know that hiding from God is not the answer. We must and *can* meet God face-to-face. Because of our faith in Jesus, we "dare to have the boldness (courage and confidence) of free access (an unreserved approach to God with freedom and without fear)" (Ephesians 3:12 AMP).

This life in Christ is to be lived to the fullest, not in partial victories and agonizing defeats. We are not to live as Hagars, slaves to sin, but as free women like Sarah. For once she trusted God to deliver as promised, He brought her laughter.

> *The Lord came to help Sarah and did for her what he had promised. So she became pregnant, and at the exact time God had promised, she gave birth to a son for Abraham in his old age. . . . Sarah said, "God has brought me laughter, and everyone who hears about this will laugh with me."*

GENESIS 21:1–2, 6 GW

Once Sarah banished fear and doubt, once she stopped trying to fix things herself, once she "let go and let God," His promises became her reality, and she was overjoyed!

But where's the proof that Jesus came to save us? That He is all-powerful? That we are more than conquerors through Him? That because of all He has done for us, we are to be filled with joy? To find the answers, we bring our thirsty hearts, minds, and souls to the source, the well of God's Word.

Here we find proof that Jesus did come to save us. The angel of the Lord appeared to Joseph in a dream with the first birth announcement: "After her baby is born, name him Jesus, because he will save his people from their sins" (Matthew 1:21 CEV). Later an angel came to the shepherds, saying, "I am bringing you good news that will be a great joy to all the people. Today your Savior was born in the town of David. He is Christ, the Lord" (Luke 2:10–11 NCV).

We look to Zacharias. Filled with the Holy Spirit, he "prophesied. . .that we being delivered out of the hand of our enemies might serve him without fear, in holiness and righteousness before him, all the days of our life" (Luke 1:67, 74–75 KJV).

Later, Paul told Titus, "The grace of God (His unmerited favor and blessing) has come forward (appeared) for the deliverance from sin and the eternal salvation for all mankind" (Titus 2:11 AMP). (See also Acts 3:26; Ephesians 5:26–27; Titus 2:12, 14; 1 Peter 2:21–22, 24; Ephesians 4:22–24.)

Hannah Whitall Smith wrote, "The redemption accomplished for us by our Lord Jesus Christ on the cross at Calvary is a redemption from the power of sin as well as from its guilt. He is able to save to the uttermost all who come unto God by Him."

Christians can be joyful because we are saved—not because we don't sin. We still miss the mark. But we can find our joy in believing that our debt for sin has been paid in full—through the death of Jesus on the cross.

> *You were once dead because of your failures and your uncircumcised corrupt*
> *nature. But God made you alive with Christ when he forgave all our failures.*
> *He did this by erasing the charges that were brought against us by the written*
> *laws God had established. He took the charges away by nailing them to the cross.*
> COLOSSIANS 2:13–14 GW

We rejoice because that sin, the obstacle standing between us and God, has been expunged from our record. "And in addition to everything else, we are happy because God sent our Lord Jesus Christ to make peace with us" (Romans 5:11 CEV).

But are we living as if we are saved and guilt free, or are we exhausted from trying to live the holy life in our own power? Are we hiding, hoping that no one picks up on the fact that our Christian life isn't "working"?

Here is where we need to believe that we have the power of the One who calmed the sea and stopped the wind. Paul told the Ephesians, "I want you to know about the great and mighty power that God has for us followers. It is the same wonderful power he used when he raised Christ from death and let him sit at his right side in heaven" (Ephesians 1:19–20 CEV).

All we need to do to access that mighty power is to let Christ live through us, to trust Him with our lives, to honor Him with our mouths. We can stop cowering and instead understand that "we are more than conquerors and gain a surpassing victory through Him Who loved us" (Romans 8:37 AMP). We can know that through thick and thin, "God is on our side" (Romans 8:31 AMP), not once in a while but over and over again. Jesus "is able always to save those who come to God through him because he always lives, asking God to help them" (Hebrews 7:25 NCV). We needn't have any fear at any time! That alone should bring joy and peace into our hearts!

So we know that in Jesus we are saved, we have access to power, and we are more than conquerors. Where then does an expectation or promise of joy come in?

It comes in Christ! It comes in trusting Him, applying His Word to our lives, living out our faith. It's not that there will be no trials. We might lose a job, a house, a husband, a child; we will have sickness, dashed hopes, and unmet expectations. Jesus Himself was disappointed with people, including His own disciples at times. He displayed His anger with the money changers and religious leaders of His day. He, too, suffered His share of loss and wept for Lazarus. But He also had the joy of a deep relationship with His Father God. Like Jesus, we, too, are children of Father God, and because we are His, He has "sent forth the Spirit of His Son into [our] hearts, crying out, 'Abba [an Aramaic term meaning *Daddy*]' " (Galatians 4:6 NKJV). By following in Jesus' steps, walking as He walked, we can have the same joyous relationship with Father God.

As good and faithful servants, we can "come and share [our Master's] joy" (Matthew 25:23 NCV). Jesus wants us to have the same joy He has so that our joy will be as full as it can be (see John 15:11 NCV). All we need to do is "ask and. . .receive, so that [our] joy will be the fullest possible joy" (John 16:24 NCV).

We can have joy even when we suffer, because like Jesus, we know "that these troubles produce patience" (Romans 5:3 NCV). In fact, "in the kingdom of God"—the place where we desire to live, breathe, and serve—"the important things are living right with God, peace, and joy in the Holy Spirit" (Romans 14:17 NCV). These are the prerequisites if we deem to live in a palace instead of a spiritual-pauper's house.

So we *can* and *should expect* joy in this life. If we don't have joy, we are not maturing in our faith. Paul wrote to the Philippians, "I am convinced that I will remain alive so I can continue to help all of you grow and experience the joy of your faith" (Philippians 1:25 NLT). He exhorted his readers to "always be full of joy in the Lord. I say it again—rejoice!" (Philippians 4:4 NLT).

"Just as Christ was raised from the dead by the glorious power of the Father, now we also may live new lives" (Romans 6:4 NLT)—if we can trust God to deliver us no matter what our circumstances. We are new women in Christ whether or not we feel like it. Available to us are love, forgiveness, peace, and joy in Christ—if we stop sweeping our sins under the rug and, mired by guilt, shrinking from His presence.

In Christ we have "a friend who sticks closer than a brother" (Proverbs 18:24 NKJV). Yes, ladies, we have a "big brother" who can and will defend us against all enemies, look out for us, size up our situations, and advise us. He loves us like no other, shielding us from evil, taking on all challengers, gladly bearing our burdens. When others disappoint, discourage, depress, or desert us, He stands by our sides. He watches over us as we sleep, guarding the gates. What joy His constant presence gives us! But we must be *aware* of His presence—within and without, above and below, to the right and the left.

Because of His sacrifice for us, we can call our Father God *Abba*! And we can be assured of the Holy Spirit's comfort and guidance.

Tell your brother Jesus all of your troubles, including sins. Tell Him you want to do better. Call on Christ's death-defying power. Count on God's protection. Follow the Holy Spirit's guidance. Sing a new song of joy unto the Lord who sees us as His dear daughters. Dance in celebration of Christ's saving grace and power.

> *Weeping may last for the night, but there is a song of joy in the morning. . . . You have changed my sobbing into dancing. You have removed my sackcloth and clothed me with joy so that my soul may praise you with music and not be silent.*
>
> PSALM 30:5, 11–12 GW

Remember that no one can take your joy away from you (see John 16:22 NASB). Refuse to be like Hagar, sitting down in the midst of your troubles, sobbing, allowing the weight of the world's woes to oppress you. Just like He called Hagar, God is calling you: " 'Don't be afraid!' . . . God opened her eyes. Then she saw a well. She filled the container with water" (Genesis 21:17, 19 GW). God is and always will be with you. Don't let your faith dry up. Run to His well and tap into His life-giving water.

Ask God to open

> *the eyes of your understanding. . .that you may know what is the hope of His calling, what are the riches of the glory of His inheritance in the saints, and what is the exceeding greatness of His power toward us who believe, according to the working of His mighty power which He worked in Christ when He raised Him from the dead and seated Him at His right hand in the heavenly places.*
>
> EPHESIANS 1:18–20 NKJV

"When you have begun to have some faint glimpses of this power," Smith wrote, "learn to look away utterly from your own weakness, and, putting your case into His hands, trust Him to deliver you."

In the next seven days, impress these things in your mind as you begin your journey on the pathway to a deep, abiding joy.

> *"As for you, be strong and do not give up,*
> *for your work will be rewarded."*
> 2 CHRONICLES 15:7 TNIV

$\mathscr{P}$ATH MARKERS

$\mathscr{P}$romise

[Jesus said,] "Ask, using my name, and you will receive, and you will have abundant joy."

JOHN 16:24 NLT

$\mathscr{P}$roof

While Peter was in prison, the church prayed very earnestly for him. . . .

Suddenly, there was a bright light in the cell, and an angel of the Lord stood before Peter. The angel struck him on the side to awaken him and said, "Quick! Get up!" And the chains fell off his wrists. Then the angel told him, "Get dressed and put on your sandals." And he did. "Now put on your coat and follow me," the angel ordered.

So Peter left the cell, following the angel. But all the time he thought it was a vision. He didn't realize it was actually happening. . . .

Peter finally came to his senses. "It's really true!" he said. "The Lord has sent his angel and saved me from Herod and from what the Jewish leaders had planned to do to me!"

When he realized this, he went to the home of Mary, the mother of John Mark, where many were gathered for prayer. He knocked at the door in the gate, and a servant girl named Rhoda came to open it. When she recognized Peter's voice, she was so overjoyed that, instead of opening the door, she ran back inside and told everyone, "Peter is standing at the door!"

ACTS 12:5, 7–9, 11–14 NLT

Provision

[Jesus said,] "I have told you these things so that you can have the same joy I have and so that your joy will be the fullest possible joy."

JOHN 15:11 NCV

Portrait

In Christ, I am able to have joy in any situation (see Philippians 4:4, 12).

DAY 1
Becoming His Vision

I urge you. . .by the mercies of God, to present your bodies a living and holy sacrifice, acceptable to God, which is your spiritual service of worship.

ROMANS 12:1 NASB

My Lord Jesus, I bring myself to You today, straining to hear a whisper from Your mouth, to feel the touch of Your hand, to taste the goodness of Your Word, to see the light of Your presence in my life. I am Yours to mold and shape. Help me to become what You've called me to be, to become the vision You have had of me since the beginning.

DAY 2
A New Focus

And do not be conformed to this world, but be transformed by the renewing of your mind, so that you may prove what the will of God is, that which is good and acceptable and perfect.

ROMANS 12:2 NASB

There are so many worldly woes tumbling around in my mind, steering my behavior, driving me out of Your path for me, God. Fill my mind with Your light. Help me to focus on the good things of this world—on the rose, not its thorns. For I want to know and to do Your will. I want to see Your beauty working its way out through me.

DAY 3
A Fresh Start

Now we look inside, and what we see is
that anyone united with the Messiah
gets a fresh start, is created new.
The old life is gone; a new life burgeons!

2 CORINTHIANS 5:17 MSG

Jesus, I need a fresh start every day, every moment! I long to be transformed but know I can only change with You working through me. If I try this in my own power, I will remain the same. So I continue to be encouraged, Lord, knowing that You understand my difficulties and are walking with me, hand in hand, from this day, this moment, forward! Thank You for being so patient!

DAY 4
Energized by God's Goodness

I would have lost heart, unless I had believed that
I would see the goodness of the LORD in the land of the living.

PSALM 27:13 NKJV

Discouragement is keeping me from looking on the bright side of life. Give me courage, Lord; give me hope. Help me to realize that this temporal world is not all there is, that there is a silver lining—and it is You. Energize me for the work I have before me today. Help me not to lose heart but to know, to believe, to have a vision for Your goodness in this land of the living.

Day 5
Good Bearings

The fruit of the Spirit is love, joy, peace, longsuffering,
gentleness, goodness, faith, meekness, temperance.
GALATIANS 5:22–23 KJV

I want to walk in the Spirit, Jesus. I want to bear good fruit in this world. Help me to look at others with love; to feel Your deep, abundant joy; to radiate peace to all; to suffer patiently, knowing You'll work everything out in my life; to be gentle with others; to focus on Your goodness; to keep my eyes on You; to be humble in spirit; and to gain self-control.

Day 6
Abounding in Hope

Now may the God of hope fill you with
all joy and peace in believing,
so that you will abound in hope by
the power of the Holy Spirit.
ROMANS 15:13 NASB

*Y*ou alone are my hope in this world, Lord. When I rely on things, myself, or others, I am often disappointed. So I'm fixing my focus on You and You alone. As I form a smile, I feel Your joy springing up from deep within. I experience an overwhelming peace in my heart. The power of Your Holy Spirit fills me with hope. Because of You, I can do anything You've called me to do!

Day 7
Blessed in Believing

The Lord has blessed you because you
believed that he will keep his promise.
Luke 1:45 CEV

Lord, I'm amazed at the way You keep blessing me. Your promises are solid. What a comfort, what a burst of confidence I gain when I believe in You. Thank You for all You've given me in the past, all You're giving me today, and all You've planned for me tomorrow. You are eternal and so is Your goodness. I bow to You today, knowing that all good things come from You—and they are many!

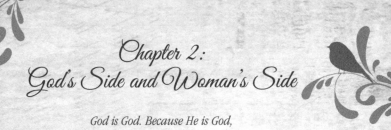

Chapter 2:
God's Side and Woman's Side

God is God. Because He is God,
He is worthy of my trust and obedience.
I will find rest nowhere but in His holy will,
a will that is unspeakably beyond my largest
notions of what He is up to.
ELISABETH ELLIOT

....

*I*n regard to the subject of God transforming us into the image of His Son, Jesus Christ, there are two sides—God's side and woman's side. Simply put, God's role is to work and ours is to trust that He's doing it. We have already been delivered from the danger of sin. Now God works to transform us into vessels He can use. As Isaiah said, "O LORD, You are our Father; we are the clay, and You our Potter; and all we are the work of Your hand" (Isaiah 64:8 NKJV).

God has given us the Word to live by. He has given us the power of prayer. He has told us that He loves us. And now we are to be further shaped—by His transforming power—from lumps of clay into vessels "unto honour, sanctified, and meet for the master's use, and prepared unto every good work" (2 Timothy 2:21 KJV).

We have been pulled up out of the miry clay pit and put into His hands. Overjoyed at our coming to Him, He begins to shift our shapes, to pull us apart, to knead us, to mold us. Our role is to remain still, patient, and pliable. Then like all potters, He puts His clay upon the wheel, spinning us, wetting us, continually turning us until He is satisfied with our new shapes and smoothes us down. We are put into the furnace and baked until we are exactly what He envisioned us to be. As clay, we are not expected to do the Potter's work but simply to yield ourselves up to His working. But in order to trust the Potter to do with us what He will, we must firmly believe in Him and the process.

For as soon as we doubt and lose our focus, we begin to sink.

Remember the effect of Peter's doubt? When Jesus, walking on the water, came to His boatload of fearful followers, they cried out.

> *But Jesus quickly spoke to them, "Have courage! It is I. Do not be afraid."*
> *Peter said, "Lord, if it is really you, then command me to come to you on the water."*
> *Jesus said, "Come."*
> *And Peter left the boat and walked on the water to Jesus. But when Peter saw the wind and the waves, he became afraid and began to sink. He shouted, "Lord, save me!" Immediately Jesus reached out his hand and caught Peter. Jesus said, "Your faith is small. Why did you doubt?"*
>
> MATTHEW 14:27–31 NCV

When we step out of the boat and head to Jesus' side, we are putting ourselves in His hands. But when we look away from Him and stare at the wind and waves, we are no longer trusting in or focusing on Jesus. Then, like Peter, we begin to sink. It's as if we have taken ourselves out of the Potter's hands and retreated back into our clay pits. No longer surrendering ourselves to the Potter's skill, we obstruct the work of the Master Creator and so remain lumps of clay instead of transforming into beautiful vessels.

When there is no faith, there is no trust and no transforming work can be done. Consider the lack of faith in Jesus' own hometown, where "he did not many mighty works there because of their unbelief" (Matthew 13:58 KJV). *Matthew Henry's Commentary* says that their lack of belief did, "in effect, tie [Jesus'] hands. . . . Unbelief is the great obstruction to Christ's favours. So that if mighty works be not wrought in us, it is not for want of power or grace in Christ, but for want of faith in us."

God forbid we should be found wanting and remain lumps of clay. Or that we miss out on the grand plans God has in store for us because we've sunk down into the dark and deep blue sea!

Are we to be like Sarah, who laughed when God said she would be a mother even in her old age? Her unbelief prompted God to censure her and ask, "Is any thing too hard for the Lord?" (Genesis 18:14 KJV).

When Jairus, one of the rulers of the synagogue, came to Jesus, he was filled with faith and begged Jesus to heal his young daughter, who was dying. Jesus agreed to do so. As He walked with Jairus toward Jairus's home, some people came from the house, saying, "Your daughter is dead. Why trouble the Teacher any further?" (Mark 5:35 NKJV). But Jesus reassured Jairus with some of the sweetest words: "Do not be afraid; only believe" (Mark 5:36 NKJV).

By the time Jesus got to Jairus's house, a myriad of mourners were there, weeping and wailing. Jesus told them, "The child is not dead, but sleeping" (Mark 5:39 NKJV). They merely laughed at Him.

So Jesus had them all driven out of the house. Taking with Him Peter, James, and John as well as the child's parents, He went to the little girl's bedside and ordered her to rise. That instant, she got up and began walking around.

What an awesome example of how Jesus works when we believe! Dare we miss the miracles He can perform, the amazing way He can transform us—who can then in turn transform the world around us? How can we not trust and surrender our lives to the power of Christ? How can we not put ourselves into His capable hands and expect to become beautiful vessels, inside and out?

Hannah Whitall Smith wrote:

All that we claim, then, in this life of sanctification is that by an act of faith we put ourselves into the hands of the Lord, for Him to work in us all the good pleasure of His will, and then, by a continuous exercise of faith, keep ourselves there. When we do it, and while we do it, we are, in the scriptural sense, truly pleasing to God, although it may require years of training and discipline to mature us into a vessel that shall be in all respects to His honor and fitted to every good work.

We lumps of clay will not be transformed into vessels overnight. It will take many spins of the Potter's wheel. But we can rest assured that we are safer in His hands than in a deep, dark pit, that although we may experience growing pains, we will someday be mature Christians, energized and transformed by the Holy Spirit.

Sarah took herself out of God's hands when she became impatient while waiting to see His promise come to pass. She believed that God needed her to provide the solution. Edith Deen wrote in *All the Women of the Bible* that "not understanding the divine delay" of Abraham's promised son, an impatient Sarah "concluded she was the obstacle." Sarah ended up giving her servant Hagar to Abraham. In doing so, she created a volatile situation between Hagar's son, Ishmael, and Sarah's son, Isaac, a decision that to this day has repercussions in the Middle East.

May we not be so bold and impatient as Sarah but humble ourselves and allow God time to work us into shapely vessels for Him. And although it is God who is actually doing the work of transformation as we yield ourselves to Him, we are to keep up our faith and belief that He is indeed doing so. To shore up that trust in Him, we can turn to God's Word and embed it in our hearts. We can lift our faith by practicing prayer and find ourselves buoyed by remaining in His presence.

Instead of being like Martha, who, "worried and troubled about many things," was "distracted with much serving," we can, like Mary, set ourselves down at Jesus' feet, listening to His every word—"the one thing" needed (Luke 10:40–42 NKJV). When we do so, Jesus will commend each of us because we have "chosen that good part, which will not be taken away" (Luke 10:42 NKJV).

Paul, writing to the Galatians, said:

> *People won't receive God's approval because of their own efforts. . . .*
> *Christ came so that we could receive God's approval because of faith. . . .*
>
> *In our spiritual nature, faith causes us to wait eagerly for the confidence that comes with God's approval. . . . What matters is a faith that expresses itself through love. . . . What matters is being a new creation.*
>
> GALATIANS 2:16; 3:24; 5:5–6; 6:15 GW

Thus we need not stress ourselves out with trying to help God transform us. That's like the batter attempting to help the baker make it into a cake. It just doesn't happen. All the batter can do is keep on trusting and surrendering to the baker. We also need not try to tell our Creator what we think we should be and do. In effect, it's out of our hands and in God's. And thank God for that! It takes all the pressure off because the stress to perform is removed.

Madame Jeanne Guyon wrote, "It is a great truth, wonderful as it is undeniable, that all our happiness—temporal, spiritual, and eternal—consists in one thing; namely, in resigning ourselves to God, and in leaving ourselves with Him, to do with us and in us just as He pleases."

Our transformation is all part of God's process. But can we be patient in this I-want-it-now society? John Ortberg wrote that "biblically, waiting is not just something we have to do until we get what we want. Waiting is part of the process of becoming what God wants us to be."

At the outset of writing this book, getting the words to come out of my mind and appear on the blank sheet of paper was a major struggle. Doubts about my ability, my vision, my career, my talent entered in. I began expending all of my energy just to sit down at my computer and stare at a blank screen. Two weeks later, worn and weary and without much progress, I went to Sunday services at my church. Pastor Chad Hogue's words broke into my heart as he said, "The way we are is not the way God wanted us to be. . . . He will give you the strength and motivation to be everything God has called you to be." Pastor Chad then invited those needing prayer and strength to come to the altar and bow to God's process.

Humbled and weary, I stumbled to the altar. On my knees, head bowed, I surrendered everything to God once again. I sobbed, my thoughts laid out before my Master. I gave myself up to Him—mind, body, spirit, and soul. In doing so, I became reenergized to do His will, to work His way. The "peace of God, which passeth all understanding" (Philippians 4:7 KJV), fell upon me once again. On my knees, I realized how far I'd drifted away from God recently, how I was trying to accomplish His feats in my own power. And amazingly enough, since then the words have been streaming into me and out onto the page.

Have you drifted out of the Potter's hands? Has impatience driven you to work in your own power? If so, surrender yourself on the altar. Put yourself back into God's hands and await His working in your life. He will transform you into the image of

Christ "from glory to glory" (2 Corinthians 3:18 KJV).

With our Lord as our eternal master designer, with our ongoing surrender, with our power of belief, with our patient awaiting of His working, we can be assured that God is shaping us into amazing, confident, expectant, joy-filled women. There's no telling what feats He is designing us to perform.

And our part is merely to trust, to surrender, and to follow Christ's injunction: "Do not be seized with alarm and struck with fear; only keep on believing" (Mark 5:36 AMP). For when we truly believe, we can accomplish the seemingly impossible!

With God's help, we will do mighty things.
PSALM 60:12 NLT

$\mathcal{P}$ATH MARKERS

$\mathcal{P}$romise

God began doing a good work in you, and I am sure he will continue it until it is finished.

PHILIPPIANS 1:6 NCV

$\mathcal{P}$roof

As he went along, he saw a man blind from birth. His disciples asked him, "Rabbi, who sinned, this man or his parents, that he was born blind?"

"Neither this man nor his parents sinned," said Jesus, "but this happened so that the works of God might be displayed in him. As long as it is day, we must do the works of him who sent me. Night is coming, when no one can work. While I am in the world, I am the light of the world."

Having said this, he spit on the ground, made some mud with the saliva, and put it on the man's eyes. "Go," he told him, "wash in the Pool of Siloam" (this word means "Sent"). So the man went and washed, and came home seeing.

JOHN 9:1–7 TNIV

Provision

His divine power has given us everything we need for a godly life through our knowledge of him who called us by his own glory and goodness. Through these he has given us his very great and precious promises, so that through them you may participate in the divine nature.

2 PETER 1:3–4 TNIV

Portrait

In Christ, I am being transformed into a new person (see 2 Corinthians 5:17).

MIND-RENEWING PRAYERS

DAY 1
Confidence in the Master Designer

Jesus answered and said to him, "Truly, truly, I say to you, unless one is born again he cannot see the kingdom of God."

JOHN 3:3 NASB

Lord, I seek Your kingdom. I seek Your face, Your presence, Your Word. Each day brings me closer and closer to what You would have me be. Each day I rise to new challenges, knowing that You are walking with me every step of the way. I have confidence that You are designing me for something special. May who I am glorify You!

DAY 2
A Work in Progress

Create in me a clean heart, O God, and renew a right,
persevering, and steadfast spirit within me.
PSALM 51:10 AMP

Sometimes my ego wants to take over, Lord. I want to take myself out of Your hands and attempt my transformation in my own power. But it's exhausting! I feel weak and spent. Renew my patience, Lord. Help me to persevere. Lead me to see myself through Your eyes—a work in progress—with the end goal of glorifying You.

DAY 3
Living It Out

"Grow up. You're kingdom subjects. Now live like it.
Live out your God-created identity. Live generously and
graciously toward others, the way God lives toward you."
MATTHEW 5:48 MSG

Lord, only by Your working in and through me can I handle the challenges of this world. Only because of the unconditional love You give me can I love others—even those who are hard to like. More and more each day, I feel Your presence, Your guiding hand, Your patience with me. Thank You for helping me become the woman You want me to be.

DAY 4
Growing Closer to God

*Each of you is now a new person. You are becoming more
and more like your Creator, and you will understand him better.*
COLOSSIANS 3:10 CEV

God, I was made in Your image. And although I don't understand everything now,
I will—as these days pass—know more and more about You. For now, I praise You for
Your love for me. I thank You for the kindnesses You have shown. I am grateful that
You stick with me in my best and worst of times. Thank You for growing me up
in Christ.

DAY 5
A Confident Surrender

*For I am not ashamed of the Gospel (good news) of Christ, for it is God's power
working unto salvation [for deliverance from eternal death] to everyone who
believes with a personal trust and a confident surrender and firm reliance.*
ROMANS 1:16 AMP

Lord, I surrender myself to You—not only in this moment but in each moment of
every day. I trust You to take care of me, to re-create me, to fashion me on Your potter's
wheel. I am excited about living out Your dream for me. So give me the fortitude to
keep myself in Your hands, to allow myself to be re-formed for every good work.

Day 6
Falling Short

Whenever the pot the potter was working on turned out badly,
as sometimes happens when you are working with clay, the potter
would simply start over and use the same clay to make another pot.
JEREMIAH 18:4 MSG

I feel like I fell out of Your hands, Lord. And it's not that You let me fall but that my ego has taken over. I'm trying to reshape myself, and of course it's not working out at all! Forgive me if I have fallen short. Help me not to give in to feelings, the opinions of others, or my own skewed reasoning. I once again surrender myself to You and Your work. And it's a relief to do so!

Day 7
God's Living Child

Hosea put it well: I'll call nobodies and make them somebodies;
I'll call the unloved and make them beloved. In the place where they
yelled out, "You're nobody!" they're calling you "God's living children."
ROMANS 9:25–26 MSG

I am amazed, Lord, that You would take notice of me. I am thrilled that in Your eyes I am a somebody who is loved. I rejoice in the fact that I am Your living daughter. I have faith in Your process. I have faith in Your vision for me. May I bring You the glory You deserve, in this life and beyond.

Chapter 3:
The Life Defined

Wherever you are spiritually, whatever you have been
through emotionally, you are already wrapped in the Lord's
embrace. Held by nail-scarred hands. Enfolded in the arms of
One who believes in you, supports you, treasures you, and loves you.
LIZ CURTIS HIGGS, *EMBRACE GRACE*

....

The true Christian life is best described as the life "hidden with Christ in God" (Colossians 3:3 NASB). Unlike the usual Christian experience, in which we believe and have been saved but do not exhibit Christlikeness, the so-called higher Christian life is described in the Bible as one of continual rest in Jesus, of peace that surpasses all understanding. It's calm assurance and abundant joy in the midst of trials and chaos.

But how do we live out this higher life? The key is obtaining childlike trust and faith in God, knowing that through thick and thin, He is with us and *wants* to carry our burdens. After all, Jesus has already taken on the burden of our sins. What makes us think we have to carry the load of our worries, woes, and cares about the present—and sometimes future—upon our own inadequate shoulders?

Most of us hesitate to give God our burdens because we're not sure He can handle them. It's as though we're telling God that we know better. It's as if *He* is the child and *we* are the father, always knowing what's best. That is a ludicrously fantastic role reversal when the fact of the matter is that *we* are the children and *God* is the Father— the Father who *always* knows best.

Consider the story of Jesus healing a man who was deaf and also had trouble speaking. When the people brought him to Jesus, our Lord took him aside, away from the crowd. Then:

He put his fingers into the man's ears. Then, spitting on his own fingers, he touched the man's tongue. Looking up to heaven, he sighed and said, "Ephphatha," which means, "Be opened!" Instantly the man could hear perfectly, and his tongue was freed so he could speak plainly!

Jesus told the crowd not to tell anyone, but the more he told them not to, the more they spread the news. They were completely amazed and said again and again, "Everything he does is wonderful. He even makes the deaf to hear and gives speech to those who cannot speak."

MARK 7:33–37 NLT

How ridiculous for us to think that Jesus—who stilled the wind and waves, healed the deaf, mute, blind, and lame, and rose from the dead—is unable to handle our problems. We must train our minds and hearts to believe what the hymn writer Fanny Crosby, who was blind, understood: "For I know that whate'er befall me, Jesus doeth all things well"! Notice her use of the present tense—"doeth." He is with you now, waiting to carry your load. To turn your trial into triumph! Will you let Him?

Perhaps we think our prayers are going nowhere, that God—too busy with bigger world problems—will not respond. That seems to be a small view of a God whose eyes are everywhere (see Proverbs 15:3). With His panoramic vision, He can see the solutions we cannot even begin to imagine. Not only that, but as soon as we cry out to Him, He hears us and responds with His all-encompassing love and affection.

Twenty-two years ago, I gave birth to my son Zachary and entered a whole new world of taking care of a helpless infant. Part of that care included breastfeeding. Although it was an amazing process that God in His wisdom had created, it could also at times prove to be somewhat embarrassing. I remember going to the grocery store while Zach remained in the care of my in-laws. While there, minding my own business, I heard a baby cry, which immediately triggered my letdown reflex! Fortunately, I was wearing breast shields and had ample time to get out of the store before the dam broke.

Just as women immediately respond to their infants' cries (and sometimes another's), God immediately responds to our cries for help. Isaiah wrote:

But Zion said, "I don't get it. God has left me. My Master has forgotten I even exist."
"Can a mother forget the infant at her breast, walk away from the baby
she bore? But even if mothers forget, I'd never forget you—never."

God will never forget us. He is always listening, waiting for us to share and let go of all our burdens—the greatest of which is self. Often we are so focused on our feelings, our unique temperaments, our own peccadilloes and temptations, our expectations, fears, and plans that we cannot see clearly. We allow these things to take over our thoughts, to hold us in bondage. But our selves must be abandoned to God.

Madame Jeanne Guyon, in *Experiencing the Depths of Jesus Christ*, wrote:

You must come to the Lord and there engage in giving up all your concerns. All your concerns go into the hand of God. You forget yourself, and from that moment on you think only of Him.

By continuing to do this over a long period of time, your heart will remain unattached; your heart will be free and at peace!

We are to give God all our burdens—of health, Christian service, careers, husbands, children, households, friends—everything that produces those horrible worry lines. Often we are so consumed with the worries of this world that we lose our focus on God. In this information age, we hear bad news from every corner of the world! It's enough to stoop our shoulders. But God reminds us over and over again that we are not to carry these burdens. We were not made for it. And when all we can focus on is trouble, we miss God's miracles!

We need to take a step back, close our mouths, and watch for God working. When we see where and how He is moving, we will be driven to praise instead of petitions!

In June 2012 in Ohio, high school track champion Meghan Vogel saw that a fellow runner had collapsed during the 3,200-meter race. Not only did she pick the girl up and help her finish the race, but she pushed her across the finish line ahead of herself. That is where God is working! This is cause for praise!

In 1 Timothy 1:3–17, Paul warns against false teachings and then relates his own checkered past. In the midst of this somewhat bad news, he can't help but praise God (vv. 12–17). What a lesson for us! What an example of how to pepper petitions and problems with praise!

Our vision is limited. We cannot see the future and are at times uncertain of the present. If we are not focused on or looking for God's working, our imaginations can run away with us. Soon we are thinking of the worst-case scenario, reasoning that we should, after all, be prepared just in case. Before we know it, our thoughts careen out of control. Next our emotions respond, and we sink in despair over an imagined outcome that may never be realized! Would that we had gone to prayer before our thoughts ran away with us. If only we had gone to God with our troubles and left them there at His feet.

In regard to our cares, it is not our circumstances that need altering. It is we ourselves. It is our mind-set that must first be shifted. Then the conditions will naturally be changed.

With a simple, childlike faith in God who sees all and knows all, our whole world—indeed our entire outlook—changes.

Hannah Whitall Smith gives a wonderful analogy about how to trust in God with simple faith:

Do you recollect the delicious sense of rest with which you have sometimes gone to bed at night, after a day of great exertion and weariness? How delightful was the sensation of relaxing every muscle and letting your body go in a perfect abandonment of ease and comfort! The strain of the day had ceased, for a few hours at least, and the work of the day had been laid off. You no longer had to hold up an aching head or a weary back. You trusted yourself to the bed in an absolute confidence, and it held you up, without effort, or strain, or even thought, on your part. You rested!

But suppose you had doubted the strength or the stability of your bed and had dreaded each moment to find it giving way beneath you and landing you on the floor; could you have rested then? Would not every muscle have been strained in a fruitless effort to hold yourself up, and would not the weariness have been greater than if you had not gone to bed at all?

Let this analogy teach you what it means to rest in the Lord. Let your souls lie down upon the couch of His sweet will, as your bodies lie down in their beds at night. Relax every strain, and lay off every burden. Let yourself go in a perfect abandonment of ease and comfort, sure that, since He holds you up, you are perfectly safe. Your part is simply to rest. His part is to sustain you; and He cannot fail.

The Lord Himself gave a wonderful analogy in Matthew 18:2–3, saying that unless we "become as little children," we will not be able to "enter into the kingdom of heaven" (KJV). Remember your years as a little child? You did not worry about your dinner. You knew that in some magical way when your playtime was over, a meal would be awaiting you. You trusted those who cared for you—your parents, teachers, and at times even those not worthy of your trust. As a child, you provided nothing for yourself, yet whatever you needed was provided. You didn't worry about tomorrow but lived in the now.

Yes, now you are grown, but God still considers you a child. You may remember the story of the woman who had an "issue of blood" (Mark 5:25 KJV) for twelve years. She'd spent all her money on doctors but could not be healed. When she heard of Jesus, she made her way through the crowd and came up behind Him. As she touched His robe, she said to herself, "If I may touch but his clothes, I shall be whole" (Mark 5:28 KJV). Immediately, she was healed! In the same moment, Jesus knew someone had drawn on His healing power. He asked who had touched His clothes. When the woman admitted her boldness, Jesus said, "Daughter, thy faith hath made thee whole; go in peace" (Mark 5:34 KJV). You are His daughter, and He lovingly provides everything you need—*in the moment*!

Make Jesus your security blanket. Whatever your issue—yourself, your plans, your husband, your children, your work, the world's woes, your misgivings, apprehensions, or anxiety—take it to your Lord. Reach out for His garment. By faith, allow Him to take your burden upon Him and leave you whole.

Be calm. Be carefree. Become an assured daughter of God, knowing that He will never leave you. He will never forget you. He has "written your name on the palms" of His hands (Isaiah 49:16 NIrV).

We are to live "careful for nothing" (Philippians 4:6 KJV). Let go of the past, present, and future. God has promised to take care of you. It's not a theory, but fact! Look to the lilies and the birds. If God is taking care of them, He is more than attentive to what those created in His image need, desire, and deal with, every moment of every day.

Like a nursing mother, when God hears your every sigh, whine, and cry, He responds immediately. You are His precious baby girl. Trust Him as you trust the earth to support you. You are in His hands, heart, and thoughts. It is in Christ Jesus—who does all things well—that you will find your peace and rest.

> *You will keep in perfect peace all who trust in you,*
> *all whose thoughts are fixed on you!*
> ISAIAH 26:3 NLT

$\mathcal{P}$ATH MARKERS

$\mathcal{P}$romise

Be careful for nothing; but in every thing by prayer and supplication with thanksgiving let your requests be made known unto God. And the peace of God, which passeth all understanding, shall keep your hearts and minds through Christ Jesus.

PHILIPPIANS 4:6–7 KJV

$\mathcal{P}$roof

We do not want you to be uninformed, brothers and sisters, about the troubles we experienced in the province of Asia. We were under great pressure, far beyond our ability to endure, so that we despaired of life itself. Indeed, we felt we had received the sentence of death. But this happened that we might not rely on ourselves but on God, who raises the dead. He has delivered us from such a deadly peril, and he will deliver us again. On him we have set our hope that he will continue to deliver us.

2 CORINTHIANS 1:8–10 TNIV

$\mathcal{P}$rovision

"But seek first His kingdom and His righteousness, and all these things will be added to you."

MATTHEW 6:33 NASB

$\mathcal{P}$ortrait

In Christ, I know God will provide me with everything I need (see Philippians 4:19).

Mind-Renewing Prayers

Day 1
Confident in Christ

If you are tired from carrying heavy burdens,
come to me and I will give you rest.
MATTHEW 11:28 CEV

Lord, I am weary of worrying about everything. My emotions are as volatile as the stock market. So I come to you today, ready to unburden myself. I lay my plans, my loved ones, my life at Your feet. In exchange, I pick up Your peace, love, kindness, and strength, confident that You do all things well.

Day 2
The True Source of Peace

Do not let your hearts be troubled, neither let them be afraid.
[Stop allowing yourselves to be agitated and disturbed; and do not permit
yourselves to be fearful and intimidated and cowardly and unsettled.]
JOHN 14:27 AMP

Jesus, only You can put my worries to rest, for You are the only One I can truly count on. In Your presence I find true peace. With You by my side, I can face any and all situations. With Your Word as my firm foundation, I find the power to move mountains. How wonderful to hide myself in You!

Day 3
Resting in Assurance

"Give your entire attention to what God is doing right now, and don't get worked up about what may or may not happen tomorrow. God will help you deal with whatever hard things come up when the time comes."
MATTHEW 6:34 MSG

I have decided that I'm going to stop thinking about what may or may not happen today and tomorrow, God. Instead I am going to rest assured that no matter what difficulties may arise, all is well. You will help me through the conflict as I pray my way through. I rejoice at the challenges before me, knowing that with You on my side, I need not fear anything!

Day 4
Peace in Hand

Jesus heard what they said, and he said to Jairus,
"Don't worry. Just have faith!"
MARK 5:36 CEV

*S*ometimes, Lord, people say things that are just not true. They are driven by the ways and worries of this world. But I am Your daughter, and I have faith in You. I know that oftentimes things are not what they appear to be. So I am not going to allow others to alarm me, but instead I am putting my hand in Yours and resting in Your presence. Thank You, Lord, for always being here.

Day 5
Childlike Faith

*"I tell you the truth, you must accept the kingdom of God
as if you were a little child, or you will never enter it."*
MARK 10:15 NCV

In Your eyes, Lord, I am Your daughter. With childlike faith and trust in You, I need not worry about yesterday, today, or tomorrow. With You holding on to me and loving me, I feel special. You wake me with a kiss in the morning and securely tuck me in at night. With Your love and protection, nothing can harm me. It's wonderful being a daughter of the King!

Day 6
Bountiful Blessings

*You are God's child, and God will give you the
blessing he promised, because you are his child.*
GALATIANS 4:7 NCV

Your Word, Lord, is filled with Your promises. Because I believe in and look to You for everything, I will receive every blessing You have for me. I am awed at Your love for me. I am overwhelmed with joy that You will not withhold any good thing from me. Just knowing that, I feel very blessed.

Day 7
Continual Peace

Now may the Lord of peace Himself
continually grant you peace in every circumstance.
2 Thessalonians 3:16 NASB

*E*very day, Lord, I need a new parcel of Your peace to help me through. Knowing that You continually give me confidence and assurance in every situation is incredible and quite calming. I am going to claim that peace in every moment of this day before me, visualizing You with me, holding my hand through every circumstance I encounter. Thank You for never letting go.

Chapter 4:
How to Enter In

To have a nodding acquaintance with the Creator of the universe is no small thought. But to be on intimate terms with Him is enough to give us heart flutters for the rest of our lives.
JOY DAWSON, *INTIMATE FRIENDSHIP WITH GOD*

....

$\mathcal{N}$ow that we know what the true Christian life is, how do we enter in? How do we spend our days confidently cool in the midst of worldly turmoil?

The true Christian experience is not something we can achieve by any sort of directed effort on our part. Rather, it is something we gain possession of by receiving it, as we would a gift from a loved one.

A child does not earn affection from its mother. Instead, it receives something the mother can't help but give. So does our Father God give us this life, as a gift He can't help but express to us. Our only role is to receive the good and perfect gift (see James 1:17) of Christ Jesus in God with a thankful heart.

To understand how to enter in, we must comprehend what it means to set ourselves apart to be totally dedicated or committed to God. Suppose you are a doctor with a patient who begged you to take him under your care to cure him of a dreaded disease. Yet this same patient refused to explain his symptoms. Neither would he take any of the remedies you prescribed for him. In fact, his attitude was that the only advice he would take from you would be that which he judged as making sense to him. For everything else, he would take his own advice and follow his own course of treatment.

To such a patient, you would be apt to say, "If you don't follow my instructions and advice, I can do nothing but leave you to your own devices. To be my patient, to have any chance of effecting a cure, you must leave yourself entirely in my care and follow my instructions precisely, without any objections or second thoughts. Otherwise, you're on your own."

In other words, a patient must absolutely obey her doctor or remain stricken by her disease. That is the same way we must consecrate or commit our lives to God. We must put ourselves entirely in His hands and allow Him to have His way with us—no matter how we feel or what we judge to be right! This will inevitably lead to a life of blessings and peace in Christ, for God the Father only wants what is best for us.

Yet some of us are afraid of giving ourselves totally to God. We believe He will endeavor to make our lives miserable, that He will take away all the things we love and enjoy, that all our perceived blessings will fall by the wayside.

Let's say you had a child whom you dearly loved, and this child came to you and said, "From now on, I am going to do everything you tell me to without crying, pouting, objecting, or throwing a tantrum. In fact, I will trust you because you love me, and you can do to me whatever you want from this time forward." What would your response be? To make this child miserable for the rest of his life? Would you sneer, rub your hands together, and think, *Finally! A chance to make this child suffer. I'm going to take away everything he enjoys and make him try to perform the most difficult feats so I can watch him fail over and over again. Everything unpleasant for him I will bring into his life, just to watch him squirm and beg for death.*

No! Of course not! Instead, you would be overjoyed! You would hug this child to your breast, pepper kisses on his brow, and tell him in so many silent gestures that you were going to fill his life with the best and loveliest things on heaven and earth.

Now, ladies, is it not true that God Himself is so much more loving to us than we could ever be to one cherished individual? Isn't He the One who gave us His one and only Son to save us from our sins? To save us from ourselves? In fact, He is just aching for us to enter not only the kingdom of God but the kingdom of heaven. Bill Gillham, author of *What God Wishes Christians Knew about Christianity*, wrote, "Christ's death saved you from hell *below* the earth; Christ's life saves you from hell *upon* the earth."

Hannah Whitall Smith wrote:

Heaven is a place of infinite bliss because His will is perfectly done there, and our lives share in this bliss just in proportion as His will is perfectly done in them.

He loves us—loves us, I say—and the will of love is always blessings for its loved one. Could we but for one moment get a glimpse into the mighty depths of His love, and our hearts would spring out to meet His will and embrace it as our richest treasure; and we would abandon ourselves to it with an enthusiasm of gratitude and joy that such a wondrous privilege could be ours.

Our words to our loving God must be "Thy will be done." And in order to say that, we must have faith—an essential element necessary to receive any gift. Nothing—especially that which is purely mental or spiritual—ever really becomes ours until we believe it has been given wholeheartedly and then claim it as our own precious gift.

Remember how much Christ loves us and how we cannot be separated from that love? Remember how much He has forgiven us? Unless we believe in this love and forgiveness and claim both as our own, they are not really ours. Yet when it comes to living our lives for Christ, we lose sight of these principles and think that once we're saved and forgiven, we need to live by works and effort. Instead of *receiving* all that He has to offer, we begin to *do*, trying to work our way into the kingdom when in actuality we have already arrived!

It's a matter of moving from "then" into "now."

Then...	Now...	
you were "disobedient to God"	you have "obtained mercy	Romans 11:30 NKJV
"you therefore have received Christ Jesus the Lord" in faith	"walk in him" by faith	Colossians 2:6 NKJV
"Christ Jesus has set you free from the law of sin and of death"	"do not walk according to the flesh but according to the Spirit"	Romans 8:2 NASB, Romans 8:4 NASB
"the Son makes you free"	"be free indeed"	John 8:36 NASB
from the bondage of sins you were "striving to please men"	seek to please "God who examines our hearts"	Galatians 1:10 NASB, 1 Thess. 2:4 NASB

Then...	Now...	
you were "strangers and foreigners"	"fellow citizens with the saints and members of the household of God"	Ephesians 2:19 NKJV
you "were alientated and enemies in your mind by wicked works"	"He has reconciled in the body of His flesh through death, to present you holy, and blameless, and above reproach in His sight"	Colossians 1:21–22 NKJV
you supposed that "godliness is a means of gain"	you know that "godliness with contentment is great gain"	1 Timothy 6:5–6 NKJV
Christ lifted you "up also out of an horrible pit"	you are "set. . .down in highest heaven in company with Jesus"	Psalm 40:2 KJV, Ephesians 2:6 MSG
"by grace you have been saved through faith, and that not of yourselves; it is the gift of God"	"according to your faith let it be to you"	Ephesians 2:8 NKJV, Matthew 9:29 NKJV
"you were once darkness"	"you are light in the Lord. Walk as children of light"	Ephesians 5:8 NKJV

Sisters in Christ, how we will live in Christ is "according to our faith." That has always been the limit and the rule. And this faith must be a present—now—faith.

Smith wrote, "No faith that looks for a future deliverance from the power of sin will ever lead a soul into the life we are describing. Perhaps no four words in the language have more meaning in them than the following." Repeat these words over and over again—not only with your voice, but with your heart, with your soul, and with your spirit. Each time you are to emphasize a different word:

Jesus saves me now. (It is *He* who continually saves you.)

Jesus *saves* me now. (It is His *work*, not yours, *to save you continually*.)

Jesus saves *me* now. (*You are the one* He is continually saving.)

Jesus saves me *now*. (He is saving you *every moment of every day*—right now!)

In Christ, we taste the joy of the kingdom of heaven. He is that "pearl of great price" (Matthew 13:46 KJV), our hidden treasure (see Matthew 13:44). He is the well of living water (see John 4:14) we so desperately thirst for and to which we may continually come.

Hidden in Christ, we are led through Psalm 23. We arrive, protected and guided by our Good Shepherd. We are fed in green pastures. Immersed in still, calm waters. We need not fear anything but simply lie down in His luscious field, our souls restored as God originally planned in the Garden of Eden. What a life of rest and triumph in Christ!

The more time we spend in Christ, the more we become like Him and the closer we grow to God. It's a win-win-win!

By his divine power, God has given us everything we need for living a godly life. We have received all of this by coming to know him, the one who called us to himself by means of his marvelous glory and excellence. And because of his glory and excellence, he has given us great and precious promises. These are the promises that enable you to share his divine nature and escape the world's corruption caused by human desires.

2 PETER 1:3–4 NLT

How wonderful is that taste of heaven, that divine nature that becomes part of us as we remain hidden in Christ. To enter into this blessed new life of interior rest and triumph, we take two steps—entire abandonment and absolute faith. If we endeavor to focus on those two things, we will reach that higher life far sooner than we ever imagined possible at this very moment!

John Greenleaf Whittier wrote, "The steps of faith fall on the seeming void, but find the rock beneath." Christ is a mighty Rock on which we stand in this life and the next. So don't be afraid to take these steps of faith. With Him beneath us, we will not sink in the sand but stand triumphant upon our Lord and Master.

If you are still hesitant, remember that God, who calls you to enter the land of milk and honey, has said:

I will be with thee: I will not fail thee, nor forsake thee. Be strong and of a good courage. . . . Only be thou strong and very courageous. . . . Have not I commanded thee? Be strong and of a good courage; be not afraid, neither be thou dismayed: for the LORD thy God is with thee whithersoever thou goest. . . . Only be strong and of a good courage.

JOSHUA 1:5–7, 9, 18 KJV

That's a total of four "be strongs" and "of a good courage" or "courageous," along with three assurances that God will be with us and never leave us. Wow! With God in our corner, His courage and strength in our hearts, and ourselves hidden in Christ, we have assurance that we can indeed cross that river and make it into the Promised Land.

God can do anything, you know—far more than you could ever imagine or guess or request in your wildest dreams! He does it not by pushing us around but by working within us, his Spirit deeply and gently within us.

EPHESIANS 3:20 MSG

$\mathcal{P}$ATH MARKERS

$\mathcal{P}$romise

"It shall be done to you according to your faith."

MATTHEW 9:29 NASB

$\mathcal{P}$roof

As Jesus passed on from there, two blind men followed Him, shouting loudly, Have pity and mercy on us, Son of David!

When He reached the house and went in, the blind men came to Him, and Jesus said to them, Do you believe that I am able to do this? They said to Him, Yes, Lord.

Then He touched their eyes, saying, According to your faith and trust and reliance [on the power invested in Me] be it done to you; and their eyes were opened.

MATTHEW 9:27–30 AMP

$\mathcal{P}$rovision

For God, who said, "Light shall shine out of darkness," is the One who has shone in our hearts to give the Light of the knowledge of the glory of God in the face of Christ.

2 CORINTHIANS 4:6 NASB

$\mathcal{P}$ortrait

In Christ, I am standing firm (see 1 Thessalonians 3:8).

Mind-Renewing Prayers

Day 1
With Open Eyes

*Open my eyes so I can see what you
show me of your miracle-wonders.*
PSALM 119:18 MSG

Open my eyes, mind, heart, and spirit, Jesus, so I can see how wonderful my life is hidden in You. I want to know You, feel Your presence. I want to do what You would have me do. I want to love others as I love myself. Teach me, show me, give me Your vision. Enlighten me so that I may not be afraid but give myself to You willingly—moment by moment.

Day 2
Wholly Committed to Christ

*Roll your works upon the Lord [commit and trust them wholly to Him;
He will cause your thoughts to become agreeable to His will,
and] so shall your plans be established and succeed.*
PROVERBS 16:3 AMP

I want to roll everything upon You, Lord, including myself. I want to trust You entirely. I want my thoughts to be Your thoughts. In doing so, I fully believe that everything You have in mind for me is good. I know that in You I will succeed—perhaps not as the world defines success but how You define it. And that's all I need or want.

Day 3
The Ultimate Shield

I will not be afraid, because the Lord is with me.
People can't do anything to me.
Psalm 118:6 NCV

*H*idden in You, Jesus, I have nothing to fear. No one can touch me. Your love and presence, Your strength and truth shield me from whatever weapons this world can use against me. How wonderful to have such protection! How glorious to have such courage in You. I can face anything within the One who will never leave me.

Day 4
Love Struck!

Nothing now, nothing in the future, no powers, nothing above us,
nothing below us, nor anything else in the whole world will ever be able
to separate us from the love of God that is in Christ Jesus our Lord.
Romans 8:38–39 NCV

*L*ord, I am awed by the fact that nothing can separate me from Your love. Nothing from my past or future. Nothing in the day that stands before me. Nothing from above or below. No power on heaven or earth can keep me from Your love for me. I feel Your warmth bubbling up inside of me. Suddenly, I am not afraid of anything!

Day 5
A Special Life

[God] did not spare his own Son but gave him for us all.
So with Jesus, God will surely give us all things.
ROMANS 8:32 NCV

Jesus, I can't imagine how broken God's heart was when He sacrificed You, His one and only Son, for me. Such love is unfathomable, yet such love is mine. And surely as I remain hidden in You, Jesus, God will withhold nothing else. Everything that is good and right will be met in my life. Thank You for saving me. Make my life something special for You.

Day 6
Safely on Your Way

Then you will go safely on your way, and you will not hurt your foot.
When you lie down, you will not be afraid. As you lie there,
your sleep will be sweet. Do not be afraid. . . . The LORD will be your
confidence. He will keep your foot from getting caught.
PROVERBS 3:23–26 GW

I sometimes feel so weak, Lord. I have trouble believing myself worthy of anyone or anything. But when I hide in You, I suddenly have confidence. I know that I am safe and secure in Your presence—which is always with me. Even if I stumble, I will come to no harm. And when I lie down to sleep at the end of the day, I rest secure in Your strong arms. Help me, Jesus, to stay glued to You.

Day 7
The Mightiest of Fortresses

The Lord is good, a Strength and Stronghold in the day of trouble;
He knows (recognizes, has knowledge of, and understands)
those who take refuge and trust in Him.
NAHUM 1:7 AMP

Lord, You are my Strength and my Stronghold. I need not fear, for You are the mightiest of fortresses. Nothing can touch me here. Even better, You know everything about me. So when I begin to fret and moan, You respond immediately. You understand all about me—and still love me! So I run to You today. I hide in Your strength. And I trust You with everything I am, everything I have, and everything I hope to be.

Notes

PART 2:

Challenges

Chapter 5:
Challenges Concerning Consecration

We are women, and my plea is, "Let me be a woman, holy through and through, asking for nothing but what God wants to give me, receiving with both hands and with all my heart whatever that is."
ELISABETH ELLIOT

....

*J*ust as our soul awakens and begins its upward journey of a higher life in Christ, just when we begin to hunger and thirst for Jesus, to do right and to *be* right with God, myriad challenges begin to face us.

The main initial challenge is our feelings. When we base the truth of God and our commitment on what we feel—or don't feel—we are misdirected, thinking that perhaps we have not given ourselves over to God at all.

Since our feelings belie the truth—that we have indeed committed heart, body, mind, and soul to God—we cannot believe that He has us in His hands. "As usual, we put feeling first and faith second, and fact last of all," wrote Hannah Whitall Smith. "Now, God's invariable rule in everything is, fact first, faith second, and feelings last of all."

This rule of God—fact, faith, then feelings—is confirmed by the woman who had been hemorrhaging blood for twelve years. She had been to numerous doctors, seeking relief from her condition, but she had only grown worse. Then she heard about Jesus and took His working of miracles as *fact*. Instead of allowing feelings of discouragement and hopelessness to override fact, she resolutely and boldly sought out the miraculous healer. She "came up in the crowd behind Him and touched His cloak. For she thought, 'If I just touch His garments, I will get well' " (Mark 5:27–28 NASB). Her *facts* about the situation were followed by her *faith*! And what was the result? "Immediately the flow of her blood was dried up; and she felt in her body that she was healed of her affliction" (Mark 5:29 NASB). What joy must have filled her heart!

What a marvelous example of how God's order is fact first, faith second, and feelings last. What a woman of daring, to make her way through a crowd and reach out for the Lord's healing power! And then to admit that she'd done so had to take even more courage! Her reward? Not only healing, but having Jesus look and speak directly to her: "Daughter, your faith has made you well; go in peace" (Mark 5:34 NASB).

The way to meet the challenge of consecration, to give yourself entirely to God, is to get in line with God's order of things—fact, faith, and only then feeling.

Are you afraid to turn yourself over completely to God's will? Afraid of losing your personality, which you may have grown fond of over the years? You need not be!

In C. S. Lewis's delightful book *The Screwtape Letters*, a senior devil writes to his minion, "When He [Jesus, their 'Enemy'] talks of their losing their selves, He means only abandoning the clamour of self-will; once they have done that, He really gives them back all their personality, and boasts (I am afraid, sincerely) that when they are wholly His they will be more themselves than ever."

So be courageous. Take the step. Turn yourself over to God. Then consider it a fact that you are His. He has accepted you—lock, stock, and barrel. Allow your faith to kick in. Know that you are in His hands, that He will work through You to do His will. As the days go by, don't give in to the idea that nothing has really changed after all just because you don't *feel* it. This kind of wrestling will go on and on unless you cut it short by faith. Smith wrote, "Come to the point of considering that matter an accomplished and settled thing, and leave it there before you can possibly expect any change of feeling whatever."

Under Levitical law, everything given to God, because it had been given, became something holy, or consecrated (see Leviticus 27:28). It had been set apart. And although we are no longer under Levitical law, there is a parallel. Romans 12:1 implores us as Christians "to give your bodies to God because of all he has done for you. Let them be a living and holy sacrifice—the kind he will find acceptable. This is truly the way to worship him" (NLT). So, having given ourselves to Christ, whose one sacrifice perfected us, we are acceptable to God (see 1 Corinthians 1:30), we are *holy*—whether we feel like it or not!

Another challenge linked to our feelings is our behavior. Remember that our thoughts fuel our feelings, and our feelings orchestrate our actions. So if we do not feel consecrated to God, we will certainly not act like it. This will force you to try to *act* holy on the surface, trying in your own power to do all the things a saint should do: attend church on Sunday, read the Bible every day, pray unceasingly, love others, evangelize, and so forth. In the process, you are wearing yourself out, doing things that at times you really don't feel like doing. Or worse yet, doing nothing at all and feeling guilty about it.

In Colossians 1, Paul is writing to the believers in Colosse. Although they are misbehaving, he addresses them as "saints and faithful brethren in Christ" (Colossians 1:2 KJV), and he tells them that God the Father has "qualified us to be partakers of the inheritance of the saints in the light" (Colossians 1:12 NKJV). Thus, we are saints—pure, holy, unblemished—not because of what *we* have done but because of what *God* the Father has done for us. Paul implores:

> *Set your mind on things above, not on things on the earth. For you died, and your life is hidden with Christ in God. . . . Now you yourselves are to put off all these: anger, wrath, malice, blasphemy, filthy language out of your mouth. Do not lie to one another, since you have put off the old man with his deeds, and have put on the new man who is renewed in knowledge according to the image of Him who created him.*
>
> COLOSSIANS 3:2–3, 8–10 NKJV

Although the Colossians have been behaving badly, Paul still calls them "the elect of God, holy and beloved," and instructs them to "put on tender mercies, kindness, humility, meekness, longsuffering; bearing with one another, and forgiving one another" (Colossians 3:12–13 NKJV).

Because God has done it all and made you holy, His work is what is going to change your behavior. His power is going to change your life. Since God has already done it, why are you wearing yourself out trying to live right? And why, if you are misbehaving, are you acting as if He hasn't done anything at all?

God has given us all we need to be everything He wants us to be. It is up to us to use what He has given us to make us holy. Again, Paul says:

> *For this reason we also, since the day we heard it, do not cease to pray for you, and to ask that you may be filled with the knowledge of His will in all wisdom and spiritual understanding; that you may walk worthy of the Lord, fully pleasing Him, being fruitful in every good work and increasing in the knowledge of God; strengthened with all might, according to His glorious power, for all patience and longsuffering with joy; giving thanks to the Father who has qualified us to be partakers of the inheritance of the saints in the light.*
> COLOSSIANS 1:9–12 NKJV

Not using the power and strength God has given us is like a woman who decides to redecorate her living room. She buys a new sofa, love seat, recliner, coffee table, end tables, and lamps. She repaints, picks out new throw pillows, and installs new lush wall-to-wall carpet. When all is arranged to her delight, she stands back, sighs, and smiles. Yet she refuses to sit in the room and enjoy it. Her reasoning? "It's just for show. I don't want to wear it out by sitting in there." Yet that is what the room is designed for—to occupy, sit down in, relax in, and enjoy.

God has made you a new woman in Christ (see Colossians 3:10)! You have been designed to be what He wants you to be! And through the power of the Holy Spirit, God has given you the same power and the same strength as Christ, to be that new woman.

Being a saint, being *consecrated*, isn't based on our feelings or our behavior. It's based on the power God has given us as we have fully committed ourselves to Him. He will work through us, to help us walk as Christ did, if we just believe. For that we need faith and prayer.

To make our prayers more effective, we need to believe that God is real—even though He is not visible to our human eyes. We must believe the fact that His presence is a certain thing and that He sees everything we do and hears everything we say. This takes the faith described in Hebrews 11:1—"the substance of things hoped for, the evidence of things not seen" (NKJV).

If you are not sure you've committed yourself wholeheartedly to God, do so now. Imagine God beside you. Pray, "Dear Lord, in this moment, and for all the moments to come, I turn myself—mind, body, heart, and soul—over to You. May Your will be done in my life."

"Your emotions may clamor against the surrender," Smith wrote, "but your will must hold firm. It is your purpose God looks at, not your feelings about that purpose."

You are now in His hands, ready to receive and *use* the power and strength to do what He wills you to do, to be who He wants you to be. If you begin to doubt your surrender, your wavering faith will cause both you and your experience to be wave-and-wind tossed. So take the remedy of repeating over and over, "Lord, I am Your daughter—heart, mind, body, and soul. I give myself entirely to You. I believe You have accepted me, and I put myself entirely in Your hands. Work through me to be the woman You have called me to be. I trust You now and forevermore."

Through the power and guidance of the Holy Spirit, may this be your moment-by-moment prayer as a daughter of God. Make it a continual practice to abide in Christ. Consider it a fact that you are a saint indeed, holy and pleasing in God's sight.

"The words that come out of my mouth [will] not come back empty-handed. They'll do the work I sent them to do, they'll complete the assignment I gave them. So you'll go out in joy, you'll be led into a whole and complete life."
ISAIAH 55:11–12 MSG

$\mathcal{P}$ATH MARKERS

$\mathcal{P}$romise

"Nothing that a man irrevocably devotes to GOD from what belongs to him. . .may be either sold or bought back. Everything devoted is holy to the highest degree; it's GOD's inalienable property."

LEVITICUS 27:28 MSG

$\mathcal{P}$roof

While they were worshiping the Lord and fasting, the Holy Spirit said, Separate now for Me Barnabas and Saul for the work to which I have called them. Then after fasting and praying, they put their hands on them and sent them away. So then, being sent out by the Holy Spirit, they went down to Seleucia, and from [that port] they sailed away. . . .

And when the congregation of the synagogue dispersed, many of the Jews and the devout converts to Judaism followed Paul and Barnabas, who talked to them and urged them to continue [to trust themselves to and to stand fast] in the grace (the unmerited favor and blessing) of God.

ACTS 13:2–4, 43 AMP

$\mathcal{P}$rovision

[Jesus] has reconciled you to himself through the death of Christ in his physical body. As a result, he has brought you into his own presence, and you are holy and blameless as you stand before him without a single fault.

COLOSSIANS 1:22 NLT

$\mathcal{P}$ortrait

In Christ, I am holy, pure in God's sight, and empowered by the Holy Spirit (see Ephesians 1:4).

Mind-Renewing Prayers

Day 1
Standing Firmly in the Truth

You are holy. . . . But you must continue to believe this truth and stand firmly in it. Don't drift away from the assurance you received when you heard the Good News.
Colossians 1:22–23 nlt

Dearest Jesus, I feel treasured that You have chosen me, set me apart to be holy. Increase my faith, Lord. Remind me every day that I am Your saint. Assure me with Your Gospel truths. Plant them in my heart so that I will not waver from the path You have chosen for me. Help me be the woman You have called me to be.

Day 2
A God-Shaped Life

Doing whatever you feel like whenever you feel like it, and grabbing whatever attracts your fancy. That's a life shaped by things and feelings instead of by God.
Colossians 3:5 msg

Lord, I find it so easy to give in to my feelings. The next thing I know, I've distanced myself from You. Yet I long to be close to You in every way in every moment of the day. Help me to obey You, not give in to whatever mood overtakes me. Give me Your peace in this process, reminding me that I am a work in progress but headed in the right direction—to Your side.

DAY 3
An Issue of Trust

You were consecrated (set apart, hallowed), and you were justified
[pronounced righteous, by trusting] in the name of the
Lord Jesus Christ and in the [Holy] Spirit of our God.
1 CORINTHIANS 6:11 AMP

*I*t's all about trust, isn't it, Lord? I must look to You as my source, as my haven, as my refuge and not allow my feelings, circumstances, or behavior to decrease my confidence in what You are doing in my life. I reaffirm the fact that I am Your holy servant and that You will give me the power to live as You did, to walk as You walked.

DAY 4
An Amazing, Mighty Power

I also pray that you will understand the incredible greatness of God's power for us
who believe him. This is the same mighty power that raised Christ from the dead
and seated him in the place of honor at God's right hand in the heavenly realms.
EPHESIANS 1:19–20 NLT

I want to understand the power that You have given us who believe in You. It's an amazing and mighty power, one that I have trouble comprehending. Help me understand what You have made available to me. Help me use that power to keep myself apart from the world. I want to be with You—my heaven here on earth.

Day 5
Flooded with Light

*I pray that your hearts will be flooded with light so that you can
understand the confident hope he has given to those he called—
his holy people who are his rich and glorious inheritance.*
EPHESIANS 1:18 NLT

Flood my heart with Your light, Jesus. Help me tap into Your power. Lead me to
understand and be confident in the hope You have given me. As a daughter of the King,
I am rich in everything. And I thank You for allowing me to be a part of God's family,
for calling me into Your kingdom—all to Your glory!

Day 6
The Riches of His Grace

*"And now I entrust you to God and the message of his grace that is able to build
you up and give you an inheritance with all those he has set apart for himself."*
ACTS 20:32 NLT

If it weren't for Your grace, Lord, I would be in the dark, giving in to every feeling,
being discouraged by my own behavior and that of others who call themselves Your
followers. But because of Your grace, You see me and others as Your special people.
Continue to build me up, Lord. Abiding in You, I await the riches of Your grace, Your
love, and Your presence.

Day 7
Exclusively His

*The grace (blessing and favor) of the Lord Jesus Christ (the Messiah)
be with all the saints (God's holy people, those set apart for God, to be,
as it were, exclusively His). Amen (so let it be)!*
REVELATION 22:21 AMP

I am exclusively Yours, Lord. Not just today but every moment of every day to come. No one and nothing can separate me from You. You have blessed my life, and I am sincerely thankful. Because of Your light, my future is bright. That's a big AMEN!

Chapter 6:
Challenges Concerning Faith

You must see with the eyes of faith, beyond the moments,
beyond the situation, to your God.
KAY ARTHUR, *BELOVED*

....

*O*ther speed bumps in the soul's pathway to the joy of a higher life in Christ are the hindrances and difficulties relating to faith.

At our first baby steps in this Christian life, we may have imagined that faith would be something we could feel, such as a heart overwhelmed with belief in God when we've received an answer to prayer or an unexpected blessing. We might say to ourselves, *Now that is faith that I feel deep within.* Or we might have just had surface faith—the faith that we think we can use to purchase God's blessings: *I have faith, so I will get what I want.*

Yet most times, faith is something that keeps us looking to the Lord during times of trial, knowing that we can trust the One who knows so much better than we do. Faith is what we rely on when our pre-Christian friends jeer at our naiveté.

Faith is nothing we can see, touch, taste, hear, or smell. Hannah Whitall Smith wrote:

[Faith] is simply believing God. You see something and thus know that you have sight; you believe something and thus know that you have faith. For as sight is only seeing, so faith is only believing. If you believe the truth, you are saved; if you believe a lie, you are lost. Your salvation comes, not because your faith saves you, but because it links you to the Savior who saves.

Faith then is simply believing God when He says He has done or will do something and then trusting Him to come through for you.

In Mark 4:35–41, the disciples found their faith disturbed and their very existence threatened:

On that day, when evening came, He [Jesus] said to them, "Let us go over to the other side." Leaving the crowd, they took Him along with them in the boat, just as He was; and other boats were with Him. And there arose a fierce gale of wind, and the waves were breaking over the boat so much that the boat was already filling up. Jesus Himself was in the stern, asleep on the cushion; and they woke Him and said to Him, "Teacher, do You not care that we are perishing?" And He got up and rebuked the wind and said to the sea, "Hush, be still." And the wind died down and it became perfectly calm. And He said to them, "Why are you afraid? Do you still have no faith?" They became very much afraid and said to one another, "Who then is this, that even the wind and the sea obey Him?"

MARK 4:35–41 NASB, EMPHASIS ADDED

Do we, too, think Jesus is sleeping just when we need Him the most? Do we think He is not watching us, that He will not keep us from perishing, that we cannot awaken Him with our prayers? Does our faith disappear the moment we are in danger and panic sets in?

It's amazing how much we trust our fellow humans and how little we trust God. When we fly in planes, we trust the pilot to deliver us safely to our destination. When we head to our favorite restaurant, we expect a good meal, not even considering that the chef could serve us salmonella-laced chicken. When we pull out of the driveway, we have faith that other drivers will stay on the right side of the road and obey all the traffic laws. When we have a message on our answering machine, we believe the disembodied voice we hear is actually that of the person who left it—without even seeing him or her!

Can you imagine going through life afraid to ride in any kind of transportation because you believe all the drivers are under the influence of alcohol? Or going out to a restaurant and telling yourself, *I cannot eat this filet mignon, for I am sure the cook has put arsenic in it.* Or going to your accountant and refusing to divulge any of your finances, saying, "I know you are going to find out how much money we have, steal our identities, and run off to Mexico with our life savings"? How about not going to London to see the Queen because, having never seen the former nor met the latter, you don't believe they exist? Can you imagine not believing that messages we receive were actually sent by the person who claims to have sent them?

So how can we have faith in these strangers who are only human yet not have faith in God—the One who has power over all creation? And how can we have faith that other places on this planet exist without our ever having seen them, yet not have faith that God actually exists?

Ladies, this Savior of ours is the One who stilled the wind and the waves, who brought dead people back to life, who changed water into wine, and who healed the blind, deaf, and dumb. He is the One who Himself rose from the dead—just to save us! So why do we let our thoughts lead us astray the moment we are in peril? It is a fact that our thoughts are very powerful. What we believe within will appear without. Proverbs 23:7 says, "For as he thinks within himself, so he is" (NASB).

Because our thoughts lead us off course, we must continually look to God's Word, write it upon our hearts, and believe that He will do as He has promised. We must imprint the words of Hebrews 11:1 upon our minds: "Now faith is the assurance (the confirmation, the title deed) of the things [we] hope for, being the proof of things [we] do not see and the conviction of their reality [faith perceiving as real fact what is not revealed to the senses]" (AMP).

Perhaps you think you lack faith because you don't feel the working of the Holy Spirit in your life. In believing this you have, in effect, not only made God out to be a liar and called false the "record that God gave of his Son" (1 John 5:10 KJV), but also lost any confidence in the Holy Spirit. In this regard, the fault lies in your lack of faith in God and His Word, not in the power of the Holy Spirit.

Put your thoughts, then, over onto the side of faith. Say to yourself, *Lord, I will believe; I do believe,* over and over again. Replace every suggestion of doubt—from within or without—with a statement of faith until, whether facing triumph or trial, you stand firm in your faith. Smith wrote:

Out of your very unbelief, throw yourself unreservedly on the Word and promises of God, and dare to abandon yourself to the keeping and the saving power of the Lord Jesus. If you have ever trusted a precious interest in the hands of an earthly friend, I entreat you, trust yourself and all your spiritual interest now in the hands of your heavenly Friend, and never, never, never allow yourself to doubt again.

Would that we could be as persevering in our faith, as strong in our belief as the Canaanite woman who encountered Jesus:

From there Jesus took a trip to Tyre and Sidon. They had hardly arrived when a Canaanite woman came down from the hills and pleaded, "Mercy, Master, Son of David! My daughter is cruelly afflicted by an evil spirit."

Jesus ignored her. The disciples came and complained, "Now she's bothering us. Would you please take care of her? She's driving us crazy."

Jesus refused, telling them, "I've got my hands full dealing with the lost sheep of Israel."

Then the woman came back to Jesus, went to her knees, and begged. "Master, help me."

He said, "It's not right to take bread out of children's mouths and throw it to dogs."

She was quick: "You're right, Master, but beggar dogs do get scraps from the master's table."

Jesus gave in. "Oh, woman, your faith is something else. What you want is what you get!" *Right then her daughter became well.*

MATTHEW 15:21–28 MSG, EMPHASIS ADDED

May Jesus and others around us be as amazed with our faith as He was with this woman's! Isn't it amazing that the moment she exhibited her absolute and persistent faith, her daughter was healed? Replace your doubting with knowing. Be as this woman—substituting fretting and fearing with firm faith. Smith wrote:

It is a law of spiritual life that every act of trust makes the next act less difficult, until at length, if these acts are persisted in, trusting becomes, like breathing, the natural unconscious action of the redeemed soul.

Therefore put your will into your believing. Your faith must not be a passive imbecility but an active energy. You may have to believe against every appearance, but no matter.

When panic knocks on your door, answer it with unswerving trust in the Lord. Speak to it with God's words of faith. Reach for His calm, for His peace. Don't allow fear and the panicked thumping of your heart to drown out the words God is speaking into your life. Banish discouragement—lack of courage—for it is a major impediment to your union with God.

Just the other day, I thought I had lost my copy of Hannah Whitall Smith's *The Christian's Secret of a Happy Life*. Since I had passages highlighted and had written notes in the margins, it could not be replaced. With my deadline looming, I began to panic. With a racing heart and a troubled frown, I said aloud, "This is discouraging." After I stopped my frenzied search and took a deep breath, God spoke: *"Only if you let it be so."*

Ladies, stop your frenzied activity. Take a few deep breaths. Look into God's Word. Allow it to penetrate your spirit, soul, and mind. Write it upon your heart. As you build up your faith, peace will pervade.

Begin with as much faith as the mustard seed (see Luke 17:6). Determinedly repeat to yourself, "I believe and trust in my Lord and His power." If you are patient and persistent in this, your worries will fade, your fears will wane, your faith will blossom, and you will share in the Lord's joy to the glory of God, who will say, "O woman, great is thy faith" (Matthew 15:28 KJV).

Faith is to believe what you do not yet see;
the reward for this faith is to see what you believe.
AUGUSTINE

℘ATH MARKERS

℘romise

I assure you, most solemnly I tell you, if anyone steadfastly believes in Me, he will himself be able to do the things that I do; and he will do even greater things than these, because I go to the Father.

JOHN 14:12 AMP

℘roof

In Lystra there was a man who had been born with crippled feet and had never been able to walk. The man was listening to Paul speak, when Paul saw that he had faith in Jesus and could be healed. So he looked straight at the man and shouted, "Stand up!" The man jumped up and started walking around.

ACTS 14:8–10 CEV

℘rovision

The apostles said to the Lord, "Increase our faith!" And the Lord said, "If you had faith like a mustard seed, you would say to this mulberry tree, 'Be uprooted and be planted in the sea'; and it would obey you."

LUKE 17:5–6 NASB

℘ortrait

In Christ, I live by faith, not sight (see 2 Corinthians 5:7).

Mind-Renewing Prayers

Day 1
A Matter of Faith

And though you have not seen Him, you love Him,
and though you do not see Him now, but believe in Him,
you greatly rejoice with joy inexpressible and full of glory.
1 Peter 1:8 nasb

Lord, I long to be like Abraham, who "by faith. . .obeyed when God called him" and "went without knowing where he was going" (Hebrews 11:8 nlt). Although I have never seen You in Your physical form, I love You and believe in You with all my heart, mind, body, and soul. Lead me on to the place You have for me. I trust You with my life—today, tomorrow, and forever.

Day 2
Getting Back in Focus

Things that are seen don't last forever, but things that are not seen are eternal.
That's why we keep our minds on the things that cannot be seen.
2 Corinthians 4:18 cev

My negative, doubting thoughts are whirling up within me, Jesus. I'm focusing on what I can feel—the wind. My eyes are on what I can see—the waves. And I feel I am sinking. Lift me up, Lord. Help me keep my mind and eyes on You and You alone. By faith, I know I will rise ever closer to what You have in store for me—all that is good, all that is love, all that is You.

Day 3
Beyond Imagination

Now unto him that is able to do exceeding abundantly above
all that we ask or think, according to the power that worketh in us.
EPHESIANS 3:20 KJV

*L*ord, I feel like I have been fishing forever yet haven't caught anything because I've been trying to do it in my own power and wisdom. So as Your disciples did, I turn to You, believing You will direct me to the right spot. I know when I trust in You, my net will wind up so full of fish that I will not be able to "drag it up into the boat" (John 21:6 CEV). What a miracle of faith!

Day 4
Perfect Peace

You will keep in perfect peace all who trust in you,
all whose thoughts are fixed on you!
ISAIAH 26:3 NLT

*T*his verse is one I'm going to memorize, Lord. Then whenever I feel caught in the storm, whenever fear and doubt start to rock my boat, I can call on these words to calm the sea. I don't want to live in turmoil. That is not of You. You are my peace and love—my still water. As I fix my thoughts on You, I am filled with calm confidence—and I am saved by Your Word.

Day 5
Promises Kept

It was by faith that even Sarah was able to have a child, though she was
barren and was too old. She believed that God would keep his promise.
HEBREWS 11:11 NLT

What a miracle—that an old woman could give birth! But those who believe in You should expect nothing less! You can do the impossible! And You always keep Your promises. I know You are working miracles in my life—right now! I trust You to work everything out for the good. Humbled that You would love me so much, I thank You, God, for being in my life.

Day 6
The Comfort of His Arms

We don't yet see things clearly. We're squinting in a fog, peering through a mist.
But it won't be long before the weather clears and the sun shines bright!
We'll see it all then, see it all as clearly as God sees us, knowing
him directly just as he knows us!
1 CORINTHIANS 13:12 MSG

Lord, I can't see the forest for the trees. My mind is tempted to focus on a myriad of what-ifs. I can't imagine how You will straighten out this mess. But I refuse to worry. Instead, I will trust in You. I will not fret but stand firm in faith, no matter how circumstances seem. I refuse to go by feelings. Instead, I will rest in the strength of Your wisdom and the comfort of Your loving arms.

Day 7
The Joy and Peace of Believing

Now the God of hope fill you with all joy and peace in believing,
that ye may abound in hope, through the power of the Holy Ghost.
ROMANS 15:13 KJV

When I trust in You, God, I am filled with joy and peace. Your Word fills me with hope for today—and tomorrow! Through Your Holy Spirit, I rise up in power over the temporal, seeking the good things You have in store for me, the things above this earthly world. Because I seek You first in all things, because my eyes are on You, I will triumph!

Chapter 7:
Challenges Concerning the Will

Before Moses went up the mountain, he chiseled out
the stones on which God's laws would be written. Our hearts
are the new stones. We must bring them to God in our hands,
ready for him to write upon them His will for our lives.
EVA MARIE EVERSON, *OASIS*

....

*O*nce we saints have stepped out in faith, trusting God as we live hidden in Christ and beginning to perceive the blessings of such a union, another challenge meets us on our soul's pathway. Although we have tasted Christ's peace and rest, both may begin to wane as we wonder if we are truly walking in God's will. And if we are not, we begin to perceive ourselves as hypocrites, merely acting the role of God's chosen children, with only a surface faith. We begin to think we have not dug deep enough, we are not wholly God's—thus, we are not holy; we are nothing more than pretenders.

At this point, we have once again begun to rely upon our emotions instead of the truth of God. If we consider that the life hidden in Christ is lived in the things we feel, all our attention is focused on our emotions rather than where it belongs—on Christ.

We know that our emotions are as volatile as the stock market. When we are riding high, our life of faith seems real. But when we are at our lowest point, we feel we may not have surrendered ourselves to God's will at all. At this juncture, we must fall back upon the truth that the life in Christ is not lived in the emotions but in the will. And if we keep our wills consistently abiding in their center—which is God's will, the true reality—our emotional ups and downs will not disturb us. But how do we get there from here?

First, we must realize that when we are not walking in God's will, there is dissonance. For only when our will is tied to His, and His will obeyed, will harmony reign within us. That is when the Holy Spirit truly begins to gently guide us into right living.

Although our emotions belong to us and are tolerated and enjoyed by us, they are not our true selves. They are not who we actually are. Thus, if our God is to take hold of us, it must be into this central will or personality that He enters in. Then if He is reigning within that central will by the power of His Spirit, all the rest of that personality must come under His influence. And as the will is, so is the woman.

Second, we must again shift our will to the believing side. For when we choose to *believe*, we need not worry about how we *feel*. Your emotions will eventually be compelled to come into the harmony of the real you, the woman hidden in Christ, in the secret place of the Father!

At times, we find great difficulty in controlling our emotions, a well-known fact to the majority of females. But we *can* control our wills. So we may say firmly and continually, "I give my will to God." For deep inside, we know He *always* knows best.

Hannah Whitall Smith provides a wonderful analogy in regard to the will, likening it to a wise mother in a nursery:

> *The feelings are like a set of clamoring, crying children. The mother, knowing that she is the authority figure, pursues her course lovingly and calmly in spite of all their clamors. The result is that the children are sooner or later won over to the mother's course of action and fall in with her decisions, and all is harmonious and happy. But if that mother should for a moment let in the thought that the children were the masters instead of herself, confusion would reign unchecked. In how many souls at this very moment is there nothing but confusion, simply because the feelings are allowed to govern instead of the will?*
>
> *The real thing in your experience is what your will decides, not your emotions. You are far more in danger of hypocrisy and untruth in yielding to the assertions of your feelings than in holding fast to the decision of your will.*

Are your emotions leading you astray? Are your thoughts convincing you that you are a hypocrite, making you feel ashamed? If so, stop. Take a deep breath and rein in your feelings. Then take those thoughts of hypocrisy away, captive to the obedience of

Christ. *The Message* relates it this way:

> *We use our powerful God-tools for smashing warped philosophies, tearing down barriers erected against the truth of God, fitting every loose thought and emotion and impulse into the structure of life shaped by Christ.*

2 CORINTHIANS 10:5

Our powerful emotions are strongholds that can be pulled down by the truth of the Gospel through the power, grace, mercy, and love of God.

When we say to the Lord, "You are my hiding place. You protect me from trouble. You surround me with joyous songs of salvation" (Psalm 32:7 GW), He says:

> *"I will instruct you. I will teach you the way that you should go. I will advise you as my eyes watch over you. Don't be stubborn like a horse or mule. They need a bit and bridle in their mouth to restrain them, or they will not come near you."*

PSALM 32:8–9 GW

And what happens if we do not cling stubbornly to our own will? We will be surrounded by mercy. And we will "be glad and find joy in the LORD" (Psalm 32:11 GW). We will find ourselves bursting out in song, so great will our happiness be!

Thus, our joy will be found when we remain in God's will. But how do we find God's will for our lives? By continually coming to Him in prayer, by consistently immersing ourselves in His Word, by constantly seeking Him first! Jesus has told us:

> *Ask and keep on asking and it shall be given you; seek and keep on seeking and you shall find; knock and keep on knocking and the door shall be opened to you. For everyone who asks and keeps on asking receives; and he who seeks and keeps on seeking finds; and to him who knocks and keeps on knocking, the door shall be opened.*

LUKE 11:9–10 AMP

God does not ask us to seek His will and then go on our merry way. It is a constant, consistent practice on our part. We are to continue asking, seeking, and knocking. In doing so, we will continue to receive God in our hearts and find His will for our lives. He will keep on opening doors that had been shut!

But you may ask, if I follow God's will, how will my family, my friends, my loved ones fare? Not to worry.

And you, do not seek [by meditating and reasoning to inquire into] what you are to eat and what you are to drink; nor be of anxious (troubled) mind [unsettled, excited, worried, and in suspense]; for all the pagan world is [greedily] seeking these things, and your Father knows that you need them. Only aim at and strive for and seek His kingdom, and all these things shall be supplied to you also. Do not be seized with alarm and struck with fear, little flock, for it is your Father's good pleasure to give you the kingdom!

LUKE 12:29–32 AMP

All we need to do is seek God's kingdom first; everything else will fall in line! When we live in God's will and are hidden in Christ, we take up residence in the worry-free zone, a place where emotions amount to naught, where they become mere specks of dust floating on the surfaces of our minds.

We cannot wrestle with God's will for our lives. If we do, we will end up limping around like Jacob. But when our wills work with God's, we are indeed powers to be reckoned with! And this is amazing because it is what we were created to do from the very beginning. Before the Fall, our natural state was in total harmony with God. We're just getting right back to the beginning!

We must keep in mind that in following God's will for our lives, we may not always see the picture or the outcome He has in mind. Consider the elderly priest Zachariah. One day while he was serving in the temple, the angel Gabriel appeared to him. "When Zachariah saw him, he was troubled, and fear took possession of him" (Luke 1:12 AMP). But the angel told him not to fear. Zachariah's prayers had been heard. He and his wife, Elizabeth (well past child-bearing age), would have a son. Zachariah was to call the boy

John. He would have the power of Elijah and help turn the people back to God.

Stunned, Zachariah expressed his disbelief! In response, the angel silenced him, saying, "You will be and will continue to be silent and not able to speak till the day when these things take place, because you have not believed what I told you" (Luke 1:20 AMP).

Zachariah, now "dumb" (Luke 1:22 AMP), was given no further knowledge between his doubting in Luke 1:18 and the moment when, "filled with and controlled by the Holy Spirit" (Luke 1:67 AMP), he sang his song of praise on the day of his son's birth. Zachariah really didn't understand what was happening, but that didn't matter. He knew that after being somewhat silent for four hundred years, God was moving.

In the midst of our daily activities, we, too, do not need to know or understand all that God is doing. We need merely to take a step back and focus on Jesus. We need not fear God's will but trust Him, resting in the truth that He knows what He's doing.

So consider your emotions as merely servants and regard your will in God's as the real master of your being. When you do, you'll find that you can ignore your emotions and simply pay attention to the state of your will. Each day, present yourself to God as a living sacrifice. Trust Him to move in your life. Smith tells us to remember that we are not giving up our wills but are simply substituting the "higher, divine, mature will of God for our foolish, misdirected wills of ignorance and immaturity":

He wills that you should be entirely surrendered to Him and that you should trust Him perfectly. If you have taken the steps of surrender and faith in your will, it is your right to believe that no matter how much your feelings may clamor against it, you are all the Lord's, and He has begun to "worketh in you both to will and to do of his good pleasure" (PHILIPPIANS 2:13 KJV).

$\mathcal{P}$ATH MARKERS

$\mathcal{P}$romise

This is the agreement (testament, covenant) that I will set up and conclude with them after those days, says the Lord: I will imprint My laws upon their hearts, and I will inscribe them on their minds (on their inmost thoughts and understanding).

HEBREWS 10:16 AMP

$\mathcal{P}$roof

Paul and his friends went through Phrygia and Galatia, but the Holy Spirit would not let them preach in Asia. After they arrived in Mysia, they tried to go into Bithynia, but the Spirit of Jesus would not let them. So they went on through Mysia until they came to Troas.

During the night, Paul had a vision of someone from Macedonia who was standing there and begging him, "Come over to Macedonia and help us!" After Paul had seen the vision, we began looking for a way to go to Macedonia. We were sure that God had called us to preach the good news there.

ACTS 16:6–10 CEV

$\mathcal{P}$rovision

I am telling you nothing but the truth when I say it is profitable (good, expedient, advantageous) for you that I go away. Because if I do not go away, the Comforter (Counselor, Helper, Advocate, Intercessor, Strengthener, Standby) will not come to you [into close fellowship with you]; but if I go away, I will send Him to you [to be in close fellowship with you].

JOHN 16:7 AMP

$\mathcal{P}$ortrait

In Christ, I have access to God's will (see 1 John 5:14).

Day 1
A Realignment Job

In Christ we were chosen to be God's people, because from the very beginning God had decided this in keeping with his plan. And he is the One who makes everything agree with what he decides and wants.
Ephesians 1:11 NCV

I may not understand all You are doing, Lord, or why, but I rest secure in the knowledge that You have a plan for all of us. I am in harmony with You, Lord, ready and willing to do what You would have me do. Your wisdom trumps my erratic emotions, God. So I am realigning myself with Your will and Your wonderful ways!

Day 2
"Well Done!"

We pray that you will lead a life that is worthy of the Lord. We pray that you will please him in every way. So we want you to bear fruit in every good thing you do. We want you to grow to know God better. We want you to be very strong, in keeping with his glorious power. We want you to be patient. Never give up. Be joyful.
Colossians 1:10–11 NIrV

Jesus, I so long to please You. I want my life to be worthy of Your response, "Well done, good and faithful servant" (Matthew 25:23 KJV). I want to be faithful to You, to know You more, to be strong in all things. Give me power, patience, and peace for this day. Keep me consistent in my faith and persistently seeking You first in all things. For Your way is my way.

Day 3
No Room for Doubt!

[We] refute arguments and theories and reasonings and every proud
and lofty thing that sets itself up against the [true] knowledge of God;
and we lead every thought and purpose away captive into the
obedience of Christ (the Messiah, the Anointed One).
2 Corinthians 10:5 amp

Father God, everybody is talking at me. But I don't hear a word they're saying; I
hear only Your voice of wisdom. I am filling my heart and mind with Your wonderfully
wise Word—so there's no room for doubt or confusion, panic or fear. I bring every
thought to Christ, knowing He will replace it with Your truths. In Him I have freedom to
be what You would have me be!

Day 4
A Mountain of Strength and Praise

There's a day coming when the mountain of God's House will be
The Mountain—solid, towering over all mountains. All nations will
river toward it, people from all over set out for it. They'll say, "Come,
let's climb God's Mountain, go to the House of the God of Jacob.
He'll show us the way he works so we can live the way we're made."
Isaiah 2:2–3 msg

Oh, what a mountain of strength You are, Lord. I run to You each morning,
searching Your Word for grounding, for truth. I look to You for wisdom during the day,
knowing I can stand firm in Your will for me. And in the evening, I reflect upon the day,
seeing Your hand in and on my life. I am in harmony with You—every step of the way!
I give You a mountain of praise!

DAY 5
A Heart Check

God, see what is in my heart. Know what is there. Put me to the test.
Know what I'm thinking. See if there's anything in my life you don't like.
Help me live in the way that is always right.
PSALM 139:23–24 NIrV

*A*bba, my spirit seems in dissonance with Yours. I'm feeling stress and anxiety in my heart, which makes me think I'm listening to the enemy's lies. But that's not what You want for me, so please, Father God, give me a heart check today. Make me aware of anything I am doing that is not of Your will. Bring me back in line with You. I long for the peace of living in Your will.

DAY 6
Words of Wisdom

If any of you lack wisdom, let him ask of God, that giveth to all
men liberally, and upbraideth not; and it shall be given him.
JAMES 1:5 KJV

*L*ord, I come seeking You first—today and every day. Show me what You want me to do. Reveal Your Word to me. Whisper in my ear the way You want me to walk. My will is in Your hands. Do with it what You will. I remain Your instrument here on earth, longing for the day when I will see You face-to-face!

Day 7
Attention: God Working!

Remember the LORD in all you do,
and he will give you success.

PROVERBS 3:6 NCV

Every moment of every day, Lord, I walk in Your will, and it's awesome! I no longer give in to fear, stress, or anxiety offered by this fallen world. I love Your peace, strength, and power as they move through me via the Holy Spirit. I look forward to each day, never knowing where You will be working but on the lookout for it all the same. Life is an adventure with You at the helm!

Chapter 8:
Challenges Concerning Guidance

*God has an individual plan for each person. If you will go to Him
and submit to Him, He will come into your heart and commune
with you. He will teach and guide you in the way you should go.*
JOYCE MEYER, *IF NOT FOR THE GRACE OF GOD*

....

𝒴ou are on the initial steps of the pathway to a life of faith. You have given yourself to God—mind, body, soul, and spirit. You are in His hands, and He is shaping you into a new creature with a divine purpose. You have determined to keep your will in agreement with His. You are, in effect, trusting Him with everything. But now you may be unsure of the next step. You know God has a purpose for your life, but which direction should you go? How can you follow His leading if you are unsure which voice is His?

At this point, you need to be certain of two things: The first is that you really and truly do intend to obey the Lord in all things. If this is so, you must understand that the Father, Son, and Holy Spirit are determined to make their will known to you and to guide you down the right path—every step of the way. In fact, they have promised to do so!

*If any of you is deficient in wisdom, let him ask of the giving God [Who gives]
to everyone liberally and ungrudgingly, without reproaching or faultfinding,
and it will be given him.*

JAMES 1:5 AMP

*The watchman opens the door for this man, and the sheep listen to his voice
and heed it; and he calls his own sheep by name and brings (leads) them out.
When he has brought his own sheep outside, he walks on before them, and the
sheep follow him because they know his voice.*

JOHN 10:3–4 AMP

But the Comforter (Counselor, Helper, Intercessor, Advocate, Strengthener, Standby), the Holy Spirit, Whom the Father will send in My name [in My place, to represent Me and act on My behalf], He will teach you all things. And He will cause you to recall (will remind you of, bring to your remembrance) everything I have told you.

JOHN 14:26 AMP

With the Father, Son, and Holy Spirit on your side, you cannot get lost. You need not fear anything! If you confidently believe in God the Father, His Son, Jesus, and the Holy Spirit, if you determine to look for and expect their guidance, you will receive it. But you must not doubt:

Only it must be in faith that he asks with no wavering (no hesitating, no doubting). For the one who wavers (hesitates, doubts) is like the billowing surge out at sea that is blown hither and thither and tossed by the wind.

JAMES 1:6 AMP

God will give you guidance if you seek it in faith, with confidence that He will give it. In addition, you must keep in mind that God knows absolutely everything! So regardless of how you or those around you see confusion and loss in the path He has chosen for you, He knows exactly what blessings await. Although you may not understand His road map for you, remember that with your human vision, you see only a portion of the map. He sees the entire picture, and in His vision you must trust.

Jesus has told us, "Anyone who comes to me but refuses to let go of father, mother, spouse, children, brothers, sisters—yes, even one's own self!—can't be my disciple" (Luke 14:25 MSG). So upon our pathways, we may discover that to follow Jesus, we are called to forsake inwardly everyone in our lives—including ourselves! In other words, we may be guided to paths that those we love most will disapprove of. For this we must be prepared. We must continually tell ourselves that God is in control. He knows all—including what is best for us.

But how does God give us His guidance? In four simple ways: through His Word, through providential circumstances, through our spiritually enlightened judgment, and through the inward promptings of the Holy Spirit upon our minds. When these four harmonize, when they are all in sync, we know God's hand is guiding us.

Through His Word. If your road map bypasses scripture, beware—you are headed for a dead end. If you are confused about which path to take, you are directed to consult God's Word (see 2 Timothy 3:16–17). If the Bible provides guidance in that particular regard, ask the Holy Spirit to make everything clear to you. Then obey. Hannah Whitall Smith wrote: "The Bible is a book of principles and not a book of disjointed aphorisms. Isolated texts can be made to give approval to things which the principles of scripture are totally opposed." In other words, be careful not to take scripture out of context, just because that's the answer or the guidance you endeavor to have.

Although the Bible tells us what kind of person we should marry (see 1 Corinthians 7:39), its text does not name names. And even though it tells us how we should work (see Colossians 3:17, 23–24), it doesn't tell us whether we should be teachers, lawyers, doctors, or stay-at-home moms. And although it gives us pointers on how to raise our children (see Proverbs 22:6; Ephesians 6:4), it doesn't reveal whether or not we should ground a teenager—nor for how long! In those cases and others, if you cannot find a clear answer in the Bible, seek guidance using the other three ways mentioned—through circumstances, your intelligence, and the Spirit's prompting. If any of these tests fails, you need to stop. Wait on the Lord. Watch for Him to move. Eventually, He will give you the wisdom you seek.

Through providential circumstances. Next we can look at what's happening in our lives, the providential circumstances that have come to the forefront. For instance, you may have been somewhat content in a career, only to find yourself laid off due to financial pressures on your employer. You thought the road was clear but now find yourself stranded, not knowing which way to turn. Sometimes, losing a job can be the best thing that ever happened! For now, you can perhaps do the thing you had wanted to do for a long time. God has, in effect, pushed you out of your comfort zone so that you will be moved to do what He has clearly called you to do, perhaps years ago!

I knew a woman who had complained about her job for many years yet never imagined doing anything else. When she was let go, she was greatly distressed at first.

But the more she thought about it, the more she prayed for wisdom, searched the scriptures, and listened to the Holy Spirit's promptings, she realized this seeming trial was indeed a blessing! She is now doing the very job she loves. Yet it was a change she never would have made on her own.

If our circumstances are truly providential, God will open doors for us—we won't have to break them down. In other words, if our direction is truly from God, He will go before us and pave the way. Mary Slessor of Calabar wrote, "If I have done anything in my life, it has been easy because the Master has gone before."[1] This is confirmed by Jesus' words in John 10:4: "When he brings out his own sheep, he goes before them; and the sheep follow him, for they know his voice" (NKJV). He "goes before" to open the gate, and we "follow him."

Through spiritually enlightened judgment. The third test is to use our God-given gifts and intelligence, which God wants us to use to find our pathway (see Psalm 32:8–9). Although we are not to depend on our own reasoning or common sense, we can use spiritually enlightened judgment to find our way. For God will speak to us through the abilities He has given us. In other words, if we have two left feet, He will not call upon us to be ballet dancers. If we are tone deaf, He won't call us to be on the worship team.

Through the inward promptings of the Holy Spirit. The fourth and final way to find God's guidance is following the cues given by the Holy Spirit. If you sense the Spirit putting up roadblocks, prompting you to stop dead in your tracks—stop! Wait until all barriers are removed before forging ahead.

But if your barrier is merely fear, if you are uncomfortable about a new endeavor or direction, that may not be the Holy Spirit saying "Stop." It may simply mean that God is about to stretch you spiritually and mentally or is about to pull you back from a path onto which you may have strayed.

For years I was a church secretary and wrote monthly articles (fiction and nonfiction) for our church and community newsletters. And although I liked my job, I felt the Holy Spirit prompting me to take up a career in writing and editing for Christian book publishers. My husband supported me wholeheartedly and had a well-paying job, so the circumstances proved a perfect time to embark upon that new career. I searched the scriptures, which seemed to confirm my new path. Although I finally came to the point where I was sure this was the course God wanted me to take, I knew I was going to be stretched! Yet I also knew that if it was God leading me, He would give me the courage to embark upon the new path and would be with me every step of the way.

At the same time, you must be aware that anything that provokes dissonance of the divine harmony within you must be rejected as not coming from God but from other sources. The strong personalities in our lives influence us greatly. So do our temporal circumstances and conditions, which sway us more than we know. In these instances, our worldly desire for a particular thing may override (or threaten to override) God's guiding voice. Another source is our spiritual enemy. We all know what happened with Eve in the garden. She listened to the wrong voice, which led to her— and the world's—fall. Thus, it's not enough to feel you are being led to a new endeavor or action. You must discern the source of the voice calling you before you rush off down the path. Step back. Take the time to find the true voice—no matter how long you may have to wait. Listen carefully. Then when you hear the Spirit say, "This is the right path. Walk in it," move out (see Isaiah 30:21). When you do, know for a certainty that Jesus is leading the way, for you are obeying His command to follow Him.

Endeavor to discern God's guidance by using, along with these four tests, what Smith calls "a divine sense of 'oughtness' derived from the harmony of all God's voices." When you do, you will have nothing to fear. If you have faith in Him, if you trust Him with all, you will have the courage and strength to walk the way He is leading, your hand in His.

There is no fear for those living this higher life if they live each moment of every day under God's guidance. It is the most wonderful privilege and promise that we have been given and leads to a myriad of rewards.

"Rejoice in it. Embrace it eagerly," Smith wrote. "Let everything go that it may be yours."

Thus says the Lord: Stand by the roads and look;
and ask for the eternal paths, where the good, old way is;
then walk in it, and you will find rest for your souls.
JEREMIAH 6:16 AMP

$\mathcal{P}$ATH MARKERS

$\mathcal{P}$romise

I will instruct you and teach you in the way you should go; I will guide you with My eye.

PSALM 32:8 NKJV

$\mathcal{P}$roof

At the command of the LORD the children of Israel would journey, and at the command of the LORD they would camp; as long as the cloud stayed above the tabernacle they remained encamped. Even when the cloud continued long, many days above the tabernacle, the children of Israel kept the charge of the LORD and did not journey. So it was, when the cloud was above the tabernacle a few days: according to the command of the LORD they would remain encamped, and according to the command of the LORD they would journey. So it was, when the cloud remained only from evening until morning: when the cloud was taken up in the morning, then they would journey; whether by day or by night, whenever the cloud was taken up, they would journey. Whether it was two days, a month, or a year that the cloud remained above the tabernacle, the children of Israel would remain encamped and not journey; but when it was taken up, they would journey. At the command of the LORD they remained encamped, and at the command of the LORD they journeyed.

NUMBERS 9:18–23 NKJV

$\mathcal{P}$rovision

Every Scripture passage is inspired by God. All of them are useful for teaching, pointing out errors, correcting people, and training them for a life that has God's approval.

2 TIMOTHY 3:16 GW

Portrait

In Christ, I have access to God's wisdom and direction (see 1 Corinthians 1:30).

Mind-Renewing Prayers

Day 1
Longing for a Whisper

Your ears shall hear a word behind you, saying, "This is the way, walk in it,"
whenever you turn to the right hand or whenever you turn to the left."
Isaiah 30:21 NKJV

Lord, I long to hear Your voice whisper in my ear. I need Your guidance, Your direction. Be my compass, for I don't know which way to go. Lead me out of the darkness I feel surrounding me. Help me look away from my emotions and focus on You and You alone. Lead me on. But if I need to wait, give me patience to do just that.

Day 2
No-Fall Assurance

If you do what the Lord wants, he will make certain each step you take is sure.
The Lord will hold your hand, and if you stumble, you still won't fall.
Psalm 37:23–24 CEV

I'm hanging on to You for dear life, Abba. Keep a tight grip on me. Squeeze my hand if I'm walking out of Your will for me. I don't want to stray, for whenever I step out on my own, I always trip up. But You'll never let me fall. You are my refuge and my strength. You are my guiding light. So I'm determined to stick to You like glue and to praise Your name with each step!

Day 3
An Expectant Believer

Wait and hope for and expect the Lord; be brave and of good courage and let your
heart be stout and enduring. Yes, wait for and hope for and expect the Lord.
PSALM 27:14 AMP

I seem to be in limbo, Lord, waiting for Your direction. Right now all is unclear. But all that means is that You want me to be patient until You give me the signal. I know You only want what's best for me. So my hope and trust are in You. Show me, Lord—via the scriptures, my intelligence, Your voice, and the Spirit's prompting—when and where to move.

Day 4
Sprinting to God

Trust God from the bottom of your heart; don't try to figure out everything on
your own. Listen for God's voice in everything you do, everywhere you go; he's the
one who will keep you on track. Don't assume that you know it all. Run to God!
PROVERBS 3:5–7 MSG

*H*ow egotistical of me to think I know exactly what You want for me! You created this universe—You created me—with a definite plan in mind. So I sprint to You today. Give me wisdom to select the path of Your choosing. I trust You to let me know where and when to go. So here I am, Lord, waiting for Your voice. Speak to me. I am listening.

Day 5
Every Detail of Life

*"For I know the plans I have for you," says the LORD. "They are plans
for good and not for disaster, to give you a future and a hope."*
JEREMIAH 29:11 NLT

I love to make plans, Lord—not just for myself but for everyone in my life. And
when those plans are ruined, I get frustrated. But I know *You* are concerned with
every detail of my life. And I know You have a grand scheme for each and every one
of us. Your plan is supreme, so no matter what happens, I can relax in hope, knowing
everything and everyone is in Your hands.

Day 6
Heart's Desire

*May He grant you according to your heart's
desire and fulfill all your plans.*
PSALM 20:4 AMP

God, You have given me certain talents and abilities, certain desires of my heart. But
I'm not sure what You want me to do with them. What's Your game plan, Lord? Please
show me in Your Word the direction You want me to go. Fill me with Your wisdom.
Help me not to run ahead of You but to wait on Your every signal for direction. In Your
pathway, I know I'm safe.

DAY 7
For His Glory

For You are my rock and my fortress; for Your
name's sake You will lead me and guide me.
PSALM 31:3 NASB

I want to glorify Your name, Lord, but I'm not sure exactly what You want me to do, where You want me to go. Perhaps You want me to remain where I am. If so, that's okay. But if You want me to move out, give me the word, and I will step out like Abraham, even though I don't know where You are taking me. In the meantime, I am hiding in You, my rock, my strength, my love.

Chapter 9:
Challenges Concerning Doubts

The more we distrust God, the heavier our hearts will get. You know why?
Because, somewhere along the way, we determined to be God for ourselves.
BETH MOORE

....

Christians are sometimes called believers—because we have faith in God. We do not doubt that He exists. But many of us could be called doubters because we do not have an active, personal relationship with Christ. We are perhaps not even certain God likes us, much less loves us. We hesitate to say that we have been forgiven totally, that our destiny is indeed heaven. In such cases, we neither feel nor display the hope of the life hidden in Christ, and it seems as if we have resigned ourselves to lives of misery, bereft of joy, accepting this as our lot.

Others, assured that their sins are forgiven and they are destined for heaven, are a little further on the journey. They seem certain of their future but still have doubts about their present. They either do not believe in or are not versed in the myriad of truths and blessings God has spoken of and provided for those who believe. Or being modern women, they doubt that the promises God made thousands of years ago can possibly apply to their lives today! Instead of taking God's Word as truth, they want to witness the proof of His promises in their lives *now*. For them, seeing is believing. And they wonder why they still have no peace, no joy, no hope for their present day. So they live in the future instead of the moment.

The instant we let doubts enter our minds, our fight of faith ends and our spiritual rebellion begins. In fact, when we doubt, we are calling God, Jesus, and the Holy Spirit liars, for "he that believeth not God hath made him a liar" (1 John 5:10 KJV)! What sorrow we must give our Abba God. What pain our doubting must cause our Savior. And what barrier we put up against the working of the Holy Spirit in our lives.

Perhaps you feel unworthy of receiving the promises of God. Perhaps temptations have gotten the best of you; you have sinned to the point of believing God would be well rid of you. After all, why should He have any love for an undeserving sinner such as you? Perhaps you have undergone numerous trials that have convinced you that for some reason God has forsaken you and no longer cares about you or your life.

On my sixteenth birthday, my father died of cancer at home. My oldest sister and my mother were the only ones who knew he was that sick. So it came as quite a shock to the rest of us. Beginning that day and for many years afterward, I assumed God was angry at me, that He had indeed forsaken me. After all, my life had been less than exemplary, and the fact that God took Dad on my birthday seemed to be a sure message to me that I was beyond redemption.

Ladies, if you have entertained thoughts and doubts such as these, be assured: God came to save us. In fact, He has told us that He "came not to call the righteous, but sinners to repentance" (Luke 5:32 KJV). Smith wrote, "Your very sinfulness and unworthiness, instead of being a reason why He should not love you and care for you, are really your chief claim upon His love and His care"! What a wonderful truth to meditate on. He truly does care for and love us, and shame on us for doubting such lavish care and love.

Remember the tale of the prodigal son and the joy of the father upon his son's return? If not, reread Luke 15:11–32. We are not perfect; yet in spite of our faults, while we are still a long way off, our Father God sees us and is "moved with pity and tenderness" for us. He runs to us, embraces us, and kisses us "fervently" (Luke 15:20 AMP). Then He celebrates our return! This happens each time we stray.

Any accusations that come into our heads about our behavior and mistakes come from one source—the enemy. He brings charges against us day and night (see Revelation 12:10). And if we listen to—and believe—his case against us, we find ourselves in agreement with him. The only things then left are doubt and discouragement.

In *The Pilgrim's Progress*, John Bunyan's classic Christian allegory, the characters Christian and his companion Hopeful are facing the same dark side of life. Having been beaten and tortured, they are being kept prisoner by Giant Despair in Doubting Castle. When all seems lost, Christian suddenly has an aha! moment:

Now, a little before it was day, good Christian, as one half amazed, broke out in this passionate speech:—What a fool, quoth he, am I, thus to lie in a stinking dungeon, when I may as well walk at liberty! I have a key in my bosom, called Promise, that will, I am persuaded, open any lock in Doubting Castle. Then said Hopeful, That is good news, good brother; pluck it out of thy bosom, and try.

Then Christian pulled it out of his bosom, and began to try at the dungeon door, whose bolt (as he turned the key) gave back, and the door flew open with ease, and Christian and Hopeful both came out. Then he went to the outward door that leads into the castle-yard, and, with his key, opened that door also. After, he went to the iron gate, for that must be opened too; but that lock went damnable hard, yet the key did open it. Then they thrust open the gate to make their escape with speed, but that gate, as it opened, made such a creaking, that it waked Giant Despair, who, hastily rising to pursue his prisoners, felt his limbs to fail, for his fits took him again, so that he could by no means go after them. Then they went on, and came to the King's highway, and so were safe, because they were out of his jurisdiction.

Ladies, we, too, have such keys! Jesus Christ gave them to us! We have "complete and free access to God's kingdom, keys to open any and every door: no more barriers between heaven and earth, earth and heaven" (Matthew 16:19 MSG). So rid yourself of any doubts, which only lead to despair. Sink your teeth into God's promises. He already knows all about you. He's known you since before you were born!

Perhaps we're embarrassed, even ashamed, to admit to Jesus that we have doubts. So instead of praying about them, we suppress them. On this despairing heap, we add guilt as a sort of cherry on top, making ourselves even more miserable and distancing ourselves further from God. Or perhaps we are afraid, like Sarah, who laughed when God told her she would be a mother:

Sarah laughed to herself, saying, After I have become aged shall I have pleasure and delight, my lord (husband), being old also?

And the Lord asked Abraham, Why did Sarah laugh, saying, Shall I really bear a child when I am so old?

Is anything too hard or too wonderful for the Lord? At the appointed time, when the season [for her delivery] comes around, I will return to you and Sarah shall have borne a son.

Then Sarah denied it, saying, I did not laugh; for she was afraid. And He said, No, but you did laugh.

GENESIS 18:12–15 AMP

Do we, too, think ourselves irredeemable? Do we deny—even to God—that we have doubts in His ability to do the impossible? Look to the promises in God's Word. They are for all of us, and they never fail. "Not a single one of all the good promises the LORD had given to the family of Israel was left unfulfilled; everything he had spoken came true" (Joshua 21:45 NLT).

When you live your life outside the promises of God, you are no longer focused on Jesus. You are like Peter, sinking in the sea because you have turned your sight to the wind and water. You have taken your eyes off Jesus.

If you have doubts, surrender them to Jesus. Tell Him, "I do believe; help me overcome my unbelief!" (Mark 9:24 TNIV). He will remind you that not only is nothing impossible for Him, that "no word from God will ever fail" (Luke 1:37 TNIV), but also that "everything is possible for one who *believes*" (Mark 9:23 TNIV, emphasis added)!

When doubts begin creeping back in, do not despair. Turn them over to the Lord. Protect yourself with the shield of faith. Arm yourself with "the sword of the Spirit, which is the word of God" (Ephesians 6:17 TNIV). By reciting God's promises (mentally or aloud), you will be putting your focus back where it belongs—on Jesus. And although the doubts, arrows of the enemy, may clamor against your shield, they will not be able to hurt you.

For further defense against demon doubts and discouragement, pray like this as soon as you awaken every morning: "Good morning, Lord. You are my Abba Father. I am Your daughter whom You dearly love and have forgiven, every moment of every day—even before I was born. Because Jesus has saved me, I am Yours completely. On

Him I remain focused. I stand firm in my faith with God as my divine supplier, Christ as my rock and refuge, and the Holy Spirit as my Comforter and guiding light. In this I have peace and joy. Amen."

So God has given both his promise and his oath. These two things are unchangeable because it is impossible for God to lie. Therefore, we who have fled to him for refuge can have great confidence as we hold to the hope that lies before us. This hope is a strong and trustworthy anchor for our souls.
HEBREWS 6:18–19 NLT

$\mathcal{P}$ATH MARKERS

$\mathcal{P}$romise

"God is not like people. He tells no lies. He is not like humans. He doesn't change his mind. When he says something, he does it. When he makes a promise, he keeps it."
NUMBERS 23:19 GW

$\mathcal{P}$roof

A man in the crowd answered, "Teacher, I brought you my son, who is possessed by a spirit that has robbed him of speech. Whenever it seizes him, it throws him to the ground. He foams at the mouth, gnashes his teeth and becomes rigid. I asked your disciples to drive out the spirit, but they could not."

"You unbelieving generation," Jesus replied, "how long shall I stay with you? How long shall I put up with you? Bring the boy to me."

So they brought him. When the spirit saw Jesus, it immediately threw the boy into a convulsion. He fell to the ground and rolled around, foaming at the mouth.

Jesus asked the boy's father, "How long has he been like this?"

"From childhood," he answered. "It has often thrown him into fire or water

to kill him. But if you can do anything, take pity on us and help us."

" 'If you can'?" said Jesus. "Everything is possible for one who believes."

Immediately the boy's father exclaimed, "I do believe; help me overcome my unbelief!"

When Jesus saw that a crowd was running to the scene, he rebuked the evil spirit. "You deaf and mute spirit," he said, "I command you, come out of him and never enter him again."

The spirit shrieked, convulsed him violently and came out. The boy looked so much like a corpse that many said, "He's dead." But Jesus took him by the hand and lifted him to his feet, and he stood up.

MARK 9:17–27 TNIV

Provision

The faithful love of the LORD never ends! His mercies never cease. Great is his faithfulness; his mercies begin afresh each morning. I say to myself, "The LORD is my inheritance; therefore, I will hope in him!" The LORD is good to those who depend on him, to those who search for him. So it is good to wait quietly for salvation from the LORD.

LAMENTATIONS 3:22–26 NLT

Portrait

In Christ, I have inherited God's promises (see 2 Peter 1:3–4).

Day 1
It's a Fact!

I rise before the dawning of the morning, and cry for help;
I hope in Your word. My eyes are awake through the night watches,
that I may meditate on Your word. Hear my voice according to Your
lovingkindness; O Lord, revive me according to Your justice.
Psalm 119:147–149 NKJV

Here I am, Lord, coming to You bright and early, before my feet hit the floor. I am hoping in Your Word, Lord, knowing that is what will protect me from the doubts that threaten to rise within my mind. I know You have given me the keys to Your kingdom. I am Your daughter, so there is no need to fear. You will do as You have promised. And I rejoice in that fact!

Day 2
Carved into My Heart

But if any of you lacks wisdom, let him ask of God, who gives to all
generously and without reproach, and it will be given to him. But he
must ask in faith without any doubting, for the one who doubts is
like the surf of the sea, driven and tossed by the wind.
James 1:5–6 NASB

Lord, You know what frightens me. You know what doubts assail me and make me feel like I'm sinking in quicksand. So I ask You today, Lord, as I read Your good Word, to lead me to a promise I need to learn, memorize, and carve into my heart. I need Your wisdom to lead me into the light of understanding. Shine Your Word on me, Lord. I am ready!

DAY 3
Disappearing Doubts

Fear ye not, stand still, and see the salvation of the LORD, which he will shew to you to day: for the Egyptians whom ye have seen to day, ye shall see them again no more for ever. The LORD shall fight for you, and ye shall hold your peace.
EXODUS 14:13–14 KJV

Jesus, because You are with me, I will not fear. I will stand still, calmly and quietly trusting in Your Word. I know You will rescue me today, once again. The doubts assailing me will be like the Egyptians. Because I am hiding in You, You will make them disappear. Thank You for always being here, fighting for me as I continue to rest in You, holding my peace.

DAY 4
Like a Sonnet

Commit thy way unto the LORD; trust also in him; and he shall bring it to pass. And he shall bring forth thy righteousness as the light, and thy judgment as the noonday. Rest in the LORD, and wait patiently for him: fret not.
PSALM 37:5–7 KJV

Lord, I am committing my way to You, trusting in You and Your promises, knowing that You cannot help but fulfill them for me. You will bring me through this. I yearn for Your light. I rest in You, waiting patiently, keeping Your Word in my mind. What strength there is in each of Your promises! Your Word is like a sonnet meant just for me. Write it on my heart.

Day 5
Hope Renewed

I cried out, "I am slipping!" but your unfailing love, O LORD, supported me.
When doubts filled my mind, your comfort gave me renewed hope and cheer.
PSALM 94:18–19 NLT

Abba God, I'm slipping into doubts again. Support me with Your love—love that never fails. Remove the doubts from my mind. You've done it before—please, do it again! Comfort me with Your Word. Support me on this slippery slope. Ensure my footing. I need the cleats provided by Your promises. They renew my hope. Oh Lord, in You alone I surmount doubt and rise into joy.

Day 6
A Lifeboat of Promises

Remember your promise to me; it is my only hope.
Your promise revives me; it comforts me in all my troubles.
PSALM 119:49–50 NLT

Lord God, Your promises are my only hope. I cling to them as I tread these deep waters. They keep my head above the flood of doubt that threatens without. I breathe in Your promises and they calm me—mind, body, and spirit. They are my greatest comfort and strength. I climb into them like a lifeboat. Keep me from looking to the world for rescue. I put all my hope in You.

DAY 7
Above the Fray

Yes, and the Lord will deliver me from every evil attack and will bring me safely into his heavenly Kingdom. All glory to God forever and ever! Amen.
2 TIMOTHY 4:18 NLT

I know You will deliver me from these doubts, Lord. Every time one attacks, I feel the power of Your promises come against it. Meanwhile, I will remain in You, above the doubts this world presents. I love hanging out with You, far above the fray. Because of Your promises, I have victory! And all the glory goes to You! Thank You, Lord! You are worthy of so much praise!

Chapter 10:
Challenges Concerning Temptations

Mma Ramotswe sighed. "We are all tempted, Mma.
We are all tempted when it comes to cake."
"That is true," said Mma Potokwane sadly.
"There are many temptations in this life,
but cake is probably one of the biggest of them."
ALEXANDER McCALL SMITH, *IN THE COMPANY OF CHEERFUL LADIES*

....

There is a general misconception that once we enter the life of faith, temptations and our yielding to them will cease. Another fallacy is that any temptation—whether we act on it or not—is itself a sin and that we are at fault for the suggestions of evil that entered our mind. This inevitably leads us into condemnation and discouragement, the continuing of which can result, at last, in actual sin. Hannah Whitall Smith wrote, "Sin makes an easy prey of a discouraged soul, so that we fall often from the very fear of having fallen."

What exactly is temptation, and how does the evil one lure us into his net? First of all, we must understand that the evil one tempts us to look to him, the world, or our flesh to meet our needs. In other words, he tempts us to act independently of God. Such temptation approaches us via three channels, cited by the apostle John when he tells us:

Do not love the world or the things in the world. If anyone loves the world, the love of the Father is not in him. For all that is in the world—the lust of the flesh, the lust of the eyes, and the pride of life—is not of the Father but is of the world. And the world is passing away, and the lust of it; but he who does the will of God abides forever.

1 JOHN 2:15–17 NKJV, EMPHASIS ADDED

Neil Anderson, author of *The Bondage Breaker*, says that these channels—"the lust of the flesh, the lust of the eyes, and the pride of life"—were the ones Satan used when he tempted Eve in the garden. First "the woman saw that the tree was good for food" (Genesis 3:6 NKJV). This lust of the flesh draws us away from the will of God (see Galatians 5:16–17) and destroys our dependence upon Him (see John 15:5). The lust of the eyes—"it was a delight to the eyes" (Genesis 3:6 NASB)—draws us away from the Word of God (see Matthew 16:24–26), lessening our confidence in Him (see John 15:7). And the pride of life—"the tree was desirable to make one wise" (Genesis 3:6 NASB)—draws us away from the worship of God (see 1 Peter 5:5–11) and destroys our obedience to God (see John 15:8–10).

Notice that in each method, Satan's temptations draw us away from and attempt to destroy our relationship with God. When we allow food to rule our lives, we have fallen for the lust of our flesh. When we have a craving for material things and do everything in our power to get them, we are bowing to the lust of our eyes. And when we attempt to be our own god, to no longer bow to the true God, to refuse to seek His direction and commands, we are drawn away from praising Him and are snared by the pride of life.

The severity and power of your temptations—no matter what channel Satan has used to reach you—may be the strongest proof that you are in the land of promise you have sought. After all, when the Israelites first left Egypt, God took the former slaves the long way, around the Philistines, "lest perhaps the people change their minds when they see war, and return to Egypt" (Exodus 13:17 NKJV). But later, when they had more faith in God, He allowed them to be involved in a few skirmishes while in the wilderness, perhaps to test their mettle. It was not until they were entering the Promised Land that the real battles began.

So if you are facing a myriad of temptations, some stronger than others, you can know, oddly enough, that you are headed in the right direction and that God will get you through. All you need is to remain confident in Him, focused, joyful, firm in faith, patient, prayerful, planted in the Word, and steadfast in Christ.

Remain confident. Someone once said that in overcoming temptations, confidence is the first thing, confidence is the second thing, and confidence is the third thing. In other words, we cannot let the fact that we're facing temptation discourage us but must stand confident in our faith and its strength instead. When Joshua was about to enter the Promised Land and face many foes, God told him, "Be strong and of a good courage. . . . Be not afraid, neither be thou dismayed. . . . Only be thou strong and very courageous" (Joshua 1:6, 9, 7 KJV). And Jesus reinforces this command: "Let not your heart be troubled, neither let it be afraid" (John 14:27 KJV).

Remain focused. Do not become discouraged when you face temptations. Instead, turn away from them and look for God to deliver you. Understand that He might not do it when or in the way you expect, for He has told us, "My thoughts are not your thoughts, nor are your ways My ways" (Isaiah 55:8 NKJV). But know and understand that He will do it! Put your confidence on the believing side—God's side, the winning side! He has overcome the world! Keep your eyes on the Champion.

Remain joyful. And above all, "count it all joy when you fall into various trials" and temptations (James 1:2 NKJV). Don't be brought low in your attitude, thoughts, and demeanor in the midst of the battle. The joy in the Lord will give you the strength you need in the midst of your weakness (see Nehemiah 8:10). Want to really catch the devil off guard? When temptation whispers in your ear, start worshiping the Lord! The evil one won't know what hit him!

Remain firm in faith. Keep your faith that God will deliver you from whatever temptations you face. Believe that His promises to fight your battles are true (see 2 Chronicles 20:17; 32:8 for starters). In fact, "the LORD your God walks in the midst of your camp, to deliver you and give your enemies over to you" (Deuteronomy 23:14 NKJV). But you must stand there with Him, for "the LORD is with you when you are with Him" (2 Chronicles 15:2 NASB). If you suddenly can't find God, *you* are the one who has moved—not Him!

Remain patient. To remain firm in faith, you must practice patience (see James 1:3–4). Give God time to work. He will not fail, for He has told us that "no weapon that is formed against thee shall prosper" (Isaiah 54:17 KJV). He will help you find a way out. Do not trust in yourself, for you are not strong enough. You need the power of His Holy Spirit working *through* you (see Acts 1:8). It is God who will arm you with the strength you need (see Psalm 18:32, 37). So step aside and let Him take up the battle.

Remain prayerful. Then back it all up with prayer, perhaps not so much for the removal of the temptation but for wisdom (see James 1:5) and strength to face it and learn from it. Remember, God has a plan for your life, for good and not evil.

Remain planted in the Word. Scripture is great soil. We are bound to wither and weaken amid temptation—and in many other ways—if we remove ourselves from it. We'll also be standing somewhere in the dark and without water. Jesus' greatest weapon when tempted in the desert was the Word of God (see Matthew 4:1–11). When you feel yourself being enticed, dig yourself deep in the Word. Memorize whatever verses will help you build the strongest barbed wire fence of protection to keep the evil one from nibbling at your resolve.

Remain steadfast in Christ. Finally, be sure and steady in your intentions to stand firm in Christ (see James 1:6–8), for you can do all things through Christ who strengthens you (see Philippians 4:13). "For the LORD will be your confidence, and will keep your foot from being caught" (Proverbs 3:26 NKJV). So flee from the evil one and run to God. Hide beneath His wings. Do not walk out from underneath His protection by doubting. Stand still. Stand firm. And you will not only escape but be blessed (see James 1:12).

Although we may encounter temptations, if we are wholly in God's camp—mind, body, spirit, and soul—we will abhor them. Thus, we must especially guard against those temptations we love to indulge. For as George Eliot wrote, "No evil dooms us hopelessly except the evil we love, and desire to continue in, and make no effort to escape from." So make up your mind, now, today, whose camp you are living in, whose side you are on:

> *Now therefore fear the LORD, and serve him in sincerity and in truth: and put away the gods which your fathers served on the other side of the flood, and in Egypt; and serve ye the LORD. And if it seem evil unto you to serve the LORD, choose you this day whom ye will serve; whether the gods which your fathers served that were on the other side of the flood, or the gods of the Amorites, in whose land ye dwell: but as for me and my house, we will serve the LORD.*
>
> JOSHUA 24:14–15 KJV

If you are looking to the things of this world to save you—chocolate or french fries, a new dress or purse or shoes, riches or fame—or to the worldlings themselves, you have taken your eyes off God. You've strayed from your base camp and entered a wilderness. So remember to choose the One who has overcome the world, the One in whom you will have success and prosper in all things! Pull up stakes and pitch your tent on God's side once again!

"We must then commit ourselves to the Lord for victory over our temptations, as we committed ourselves at first for forgiveness," Smith wrote. "And we must leave ourselves just as utterly in His hands for one as for the other."

Remember that God is faithful. He's put up an exit sign just for you and you'll find it if your eyes are open. He will show you a way to escape temptation—even when there seems to be no way (see 1 Corinthians 10:13). You need merely keep your eyes, heart, thoughts, spirit, and soul on Him, and your faith *in* Him. He—and He alone—is your confidence (see Psalm 71:5).

> *Now to Him who is able to keep you from stumbling, and to make you stand in the presence of His glory blameless with great joy, to the only God our Savior, through Jesus Christ our Lord, be glory, majesty, dominion and authority, before all time and now and forever. Amen.*
> JUDE 1:24–25 NASB

$\mathcal{P}$ATH MARKERS

$\mathcal{P}$romise

For no temptation (no trial regarded as enticing to sin), [no matter how it comes or where it leads] has overtaken you and laid hold on you that is not common to man [that is, no temptation or trial has come to you that is beyond human resistance and that is not adjusted and adapted and belonging to human experience, and such as man can bear]. But God is faithful [to His Word and to His compassionate nature], and He [can be trusted] not to let you be tempted and tried and assayed beyond your ability and strength of resistance and power to endure, but with the temptation He will [always] also provide the way out (the means of escape to a landing place), that you may be capable and strong and powerful to bear up under it patiently.

1 CORINTHIANS 10:13 AMP

$\mathcal{P}$roof

The Holy Spirit led Jesus into the desert, so that the devil could test him. After Jesus had gone without eating for forty days and nights, he was very hungry. Then the devil came to him and said, "If you are God's Son, tell these stones to turn into bread."

Jesus answered, "The Scriptures say, 'No one can live only on food. People need every word that God has spoken.' "

Next, the devil took Jesus to the holy city and had him stand on the highest part of the temple. The devil said, "If you are God's Son, jump off. The Scriptures say: 'God will give his angels orders about you. They will catch you in their arms, and you won't hurt your feet on the stones.' "

Jesus answered, "The Scriptures also say, 'Don't try to test the Lord your God!' "

Finally, the devil took Jesus up on a very high mountain and showed him all the kingdoms on earth and their power. The devil said to him, "I will give all this to you, if you will bow down and worship me."

Jesus answered, "Go away Satan! The Scriptures say: 'Worship the Lord your God and serve only him.' "

Then the devil left Jesus, and angels came to help him.

MATTHEW 4:1–11 CEV

Provision

Surely He shall deliver you from the snare of the fowler. . . . He shall cover you with His feathers, and under His wings you shall take refuge; His truth shall be your shield and buckler. You shall not be afraid.

PSALM 91:3–5 NKJV

Portrait

In Christ, I am more than a conqueror (see Romans 8:37).

Mind-Renewing Prayers

Day 1
True Deliverance

"Because he has set his love upon Me, therefore I will deliver him; I will set him on high, because he has known My name. He shall call upon Me, and I will answer him; I will be with him in trouble; I will deliver him and honor him."
Psalm 91:14–15 NKJV

God, I need You! Deliver me from my temptations. Beam me up, Lord, out of this world. Set me on high; bring me to Your side. I am calling on You now. Please answer me. You have said You will be with me in trouble, and I feel I am sinking in deep. But I know of Your power. I have read of Your strength in Your Word. You are my only hope. Save me, I pray!

Day 2
The Mighty Power of God Almighty

"Be strong and courageous; do not be afraid nor dismayed before the king of Assyria, nor before all the multitude that is with him; for there are more with us than with him."
2 Chronicles 32:7 NKJV

I feel so outnumbered, Lord. I am feeling weak and discouraged. So I am putting all my focus on You. Give me strength and courage. Help me to be brave before the temptations assailing me. I am looking to You for help, knowing that You are more powerful than anything I may ever face. I'm putting my faith in You and You alone. Save me, Jesus. Save me now!

Day 3
Great Expectations

Wait [expectantly] for the Lord,
and He will rescue you.
PROVERBS 20:22 AMP

I'm running out of patience, Lord. I'm not sure how much more I can take, how much longer I can hold on. I run to You. Shelter me in Your presence. Be my rock and refuge—a boulder that can neither be destroyed nor removed. I am expecting Your deliverance from temptation. I remain steadfast in You, knowing You will rescue me. In that fact alone, I have peace.

Day 4
Stepping Back

Behold, all they that were incensed against thee shall be ashamed and
confounded. they shall be as nothing; and they that strive with thee shall perish.
ISAIAH 41:11 KJV

Lord, I am tired of trying to fight temptation in my own power. I don't know what I was thinking, for Your Word tells me You will fight my battles. So I'm stepping back and letting Your power come through me. Already I feel relief. I know that You will give me victory over this temptation and that someday this will all be but a recollection of Your power to save.

DAY 5
Powerful in Divine Strength

So for the sake of Christ, I am well pleased and take pleasure in infirmities,
insults, hardships, persecutions, perplexities and distresses; for when I am weak
[in human strength], then am I [truly] strong (able, powerful in divine strength).
2 CORINTHIANS 12:10 AMP

When I abide in You, nothing can touch me—no sin, no temptation, no evil. When I am weak, unable to fend for myself, You come alongside and win my battles. I find myself powerful in Your divine strength. I take joy in watching my enemy run away. No one can stand against You. What would I do without You, Lord? You amaze me. I praise Your name, over and over again!

DAY 6
Living to Please Him

"What does the LORD your God require of you? He requires only that
you fear the LORD your God, and live in a way that pleases him,
and love him and serve him with all your heart and soul."
DEUTERONOMY 10:12 NLT

I know that what You have done for me in the past, Lord, You will do again. You have rescued me from temptations so many times. And now here we are again. You know I love You, God. I want to live in a way that pleases You. I want to serve You— and no one else—with all my heart, soul, and mind. So help me again today, Lord. Fight my battles. Give me courage to go on.

Day 7
Access to Courage

"These things I have spoken to you, that in Me you may have peace. In the world you will have tribulation; but be of good cheer, I have overcome the world."
JOHN 16:33 NKJV

Jesus, I am again facing temptation. Turn my head, Lord. Help me to focus on You and You alone. I need the courage I can only access through You. You have overcome the world! So there is no reason for me to give in to anything—or anyone! Hallelujah! By keeping Your Word hidden in my heart, I have peace. In You, I am found!

Failure after long perseverance is much grander than never to have
a striving good enough to be called a failure.
GEORGE ELIOT

....

$\mathcal{H}$aving discussed in the preceding chapter claiming the victory we have in Jesus, you may wonder why this chapter is about failures in the higher life. Although hidden in Christ we can win the battle, we would be remiss if we did not admit that even saints do weaken at times in the face of temptation, for we are dealing with fact, not theory. Hannah Whitall Smith wrote:

No safe teacher of this interior life ever says that it becomes impossible to sin; they only insist that sin ceases to be a necessity, and that a possibility of continual victory is opened before us. And there are very few, if any, who do not confess that, as to their own actual experience, they have at times been overcome by at least a momentary temptation.

Thus, because we are not perfect, we do sometimes fall short of the standards God has set for us (see Romans 3:23)—we miss the mark, or sin. The sin we are discussing here is intentional sin (conscious, overt acts in defiance of God) as opposed to unintentional (through ignorance, with no malice aforethought). Examples of intentional sin are stealing, lying, gluttony, and adultery.

When a Christian woman embarks upon the pathway to holiness, she may find herself suddenly and unexpectedly encountering temptation and, before she knows it, swept into sin. When she, like the prodigal son, suddenly comes to her senses (see Luke 15:17), she may then be tempted to be discouraged and give up everything as lost or to cover up the sin completely. Either option is lethal to the woman who wants to grow and progress in her Christian life. The only real pathway available is to face the fact that she has indeed sinned, confess it to God, and discover, if possible, the reason and the remedy. Our divine union with God requires absolute honesty with Him and with ourselves.

When we fail, we really have no cause for discouragement and giving up. We must recognize the fact that we are not talking about a *state* but a *walk* of life with Christ. Smith wrote, "The highway of holiness is not a *place*, but a *way*." As those hidden in Christ, we are followers of the Way. When we walk out of the Way, we can immediately check ourselves and find our way back. We must be aware of where we are, hour by hour, minute by minute. If we have turned off the path, we must instantly return to the route the Father has mapped out for us and trust Him more than ever!

In the beginning we may have, like babies, crawled along God's path. But now that we are more mature in our faith, we have risen to our feet. If we fall, we cannot lie down in discouragement and despair. We must, like babies learning how to walk, rise up and try again.

In the book of Joshua, the children of Israel suffered a disastrous defeat against the city of Ai soon after they had entered the Promised Land. They were so discouraged that "the heart of the people sank, all spirit knocked out of them" (Joshua 7:5 MSG). The New King James Version relates the account like this:

> *Therefore the hearts of the people melted and became like water.*
> *Then Joshua tore his clothes, and fell to the earth on his face before the ark of the LORD until evening, he and the elders of Israel; and they put dust on their heads. And Joshua said, "Alas, Lord GOD, why have You brought this people over the Jordan at all—to deliver us into the hand of the Amorites, to destroy us? Oh, that we had been content, and dwelt on the other side of the Jordan! O Lord, what shall I say when Israel turns its back before its enemies?"*

JOSHUA 7:5–8

Talk about despair and discouragement! How many of us have felt as if we've had the spirit knocked out of us? How often have we felt our hearts melt and become like water? Have you ever cried out, "Why didn't I just stay in my comfort zone instead of stepping out into this walk of faith?" By so saying, we are in despair about not only the present but the future as well. We become immobilized, not wanting to take another step backward or forward. Our discouragement leaves us in a sort of limbo, a place where there is no growth, no progress, no future. After such an overwhelming failure—emotionally, physically, mentally, spiritually—we may find it easier to wallow in our despondency, our faces on the ground and dust on our heads, than to look up to God. But God, as always, has a better idea. As He told Joshua, He tells us, "Get up!" (Joshua 7:10 NKJV).

But what keeps our heads down? Perhaps it is the thought that God will find it hard to forgive us. In fact, He may not forgive us at all! Or if He does, it may take Him days, perhaps years, to get over it. I know that in the past, when I was hurt or disappointed by something my husband had done, it would take me awhile to get over it. I would, of course, accept his apology. But finding it hard to show affection afterward, I would sometimes give him the silent treatment—for days. Then after the wound had healed somewhat, I would begin speaking to him again. But in my heart of hearts, I still had not truly forgiven him.

Thank God our Father is not like that. As soon as we come to Him and confess our sins, He forgives! Immediatcly! There is no silent treatment, no grudge. "If we confess our sins, he is faithful and just to forgive us our sins, and to cleanse us from all unrighteousness" (1 John 1:9 KJV). *And this we must believe!* For if we do not, we have made God out to be a liar (see 1 John 5:10).

As soon as consciousness of our sin has set in, we must immediately lift up our faces to God and become conscious of His forgiveness. We can only continue walking on this path of holiness by taking our eyes off our misstep and "looking unto Jesus" (Hebrews 12:2 KJV). Otherwise, we will keep tripping up!

Once our eyes are back on Him, we can confess what we have done. Within that confession may lie our motives. When Achan confessed to Joshua, he said:

"Indeed I have sinned against the LORD God of Israel, and ~~~~
done: When I saw among the spoils a beautiful Babylonia[n] ~~~~
hundred shekels of silver, and a wedge of gold weighing fif[ty] ~~~~
them and took them. And there they are, hidden in the eart[h] ~~~~
tent, with the silver under it."

Do you see Achan's path to sin here? He saw, coveted, took, th...
Achan, who had taken his eyes off God, had intentionally sinned. D...
sound somewhat familiar? Eve did the same thing in the garden. S...
would make her wise. She coveted it, then took it. Later, she hid fro...

When we have sinned, we need to acknowledge it. We must be...
Israel in this account in Joshua. We must rise "early in the mornin...
then run to where the sins are hidden, take them from the midst of...
and lay them before the Lord (see Joshua 7:22–23). Then we can st...
them, and bury them (see Joshua 7:25–26) and immediately receiv...
encouragement, and victory, as did Joshua and the Israelites. "Do n...
dismayed; take all the people of war with you, and arise, go up to Ai...
into your hand the king of Ai, his people, his city, and his land" (Jos...

Smith wrote:

Our courage must rise higher than ever, and we must aban...
more completely to the Lord that His mighty power may the...
work in us. . . . We must forget our sin as soon as it is thus...
forgiven. We must not dwell on it and examine it and indul...
distress and remorse.

If we do not do as Smith suggests, we will get deeper and deepe...
further away from God, putting a sin barrier between us and Him.

King David's encounter with Bathsheba is another good examp...
person's journey into failure. Instead of being in his proper place, wit...

war, David stayed at home, where "he saw a woman bathing," and because she was "very beautiful to behold," he coveted her (2 Samuel 11:2 NKJV). This was, of course, Bathsheba. Then David "took her" (2 Samuel 11:4 NKJV). After committing adultery with her, he sent her back home—in effect, hiding her and their sin. When Bathsheba sent him word that she was pregnant, instead of confessing his misdeed to God, he continued to try to hide it. This led to the murder of not only Uriah, Bathsheba's husband, but "some of the king's [other] servants" (2 Samuel 11:24 NKJV) who fell in the same battle in which Uriah met his death. Not only was David's commander, Joab, discouraged at the events, but the Bible says "the thing that David had done displeased the LORD" (2 Samuel 11:27 NKJV).

In effect, David's sin of adultery led to several murders and the death of his and Bathsheba's firstborn son. The irony is that even though David's sin was unconfessed up to this point, *God still knew what David had done*! And David did end up confessing when the prophet Nathan confronted him with it.

Trying to hide our sins is like having a cavity and not attending to it. Hidden in our mouths, it grows deeper and deeper until it becomes abscessed, threatening to infect our entire body unless we have it pulled and proceed with a root canal. If we do not confess our sins, even some innocent or seemingly harmless habits or indulgences, and continue to attempt to hide them from God (an inane endeavor since He sees and knows everything), not only do we distance ourselves from God but our misdeeds will, like David's, take on a snowball effect until we and perhaps others are buried by them. Or like Peter—who three times refused to admit to knowing Jesus, resulting in denials, anger at others, and cursing and swearing—we will find ourselves weeping bitter tears (see Matthew 26:69–75).

Confessing sins is not really for God's benefit. As we have seen, He already knows what we've done. It is more for our own benefit, for our growth. For when we admit a sin or indulgence, we are bringing it into the light, enabling us to forgive ourselves for the deed done in the past, to request God's help in finding its cause in the present, and to help guard against it in the future.

To prevent failures and their inevitable discouragements and consequences or to discover their causes if we find we have erred, we must make the following words our continual plea before God: "Search me, O God, and know my heart; test me and know my anxious thoughts. Point out anything in me that offends you, and lead me along the path of everlasting life" (Psalm 139:23–24 NLT). If we do so, He will rescue us "from our enemies so we can serve God without fear, in holiness and righteousness for as long as we live" (Luke 1:74–75 NLT).

> *For once you were full of darkness, but now you*
> *have light from the Lord. So live as people of light!*
> EPHESIANS 5:8 NLT

𝒫ATH MARKERS

𝒫romise

If we confess our sins, He is faithful and righteous to forgive us our sins and to cleanse us from all unrighteousness.

1 JOHN 1:9 NASB

𝒫roof

Blessed are those whose transgressions are forgiven, whose sins are covered. Blessed are those whose sin the LORD does not count against them and in whose spirit is no deceit. When I kept silent, my bones wasted away through my groaning all day long. For day and night your hand was heavy on me; my strength was sapped as in the heat of summer. Then I acknowledged my sin to you and did not cover up my iniquity. I said, "I will confess my transgressions to the LORD." And you forgave the guilt of my sin.

PSALM 32:1–5 TNIV

(WRITTEN BY DAVID, PRESUMABLY AFTER THE PROPHET
NATHAN CONFRONTED HIM OVER HIS SIN WITH BATHSHEBA)

Provision

Who is a God like you, who pardons sin and forgives the transgression of the remnant of his inheritance? You do not stay angry forever but delight to show mercy. You will again have compassion on us; you will tread our sins underfoot and hurl all our iniquities into the depths of the sea.

MICAH 7:18–19 TNIV

Portrait

In Christ, I am not only redeemed but forgiven (see Ephesians 1:7).

MIND-RENEWING PRAYERS

DAY 1
Aware of the Misstep

Have mercy upon me, O God, according to Your lovingkindness; according to the multitude of Your tender mercies, blot out my transgressions. Wash me thoroughly from my iniquity, and cleanse me from my sin.
PSALM 51:1–2 NKJV

*L*ord, I need Your mercy. You abound in love for me, so please help me, God. Blot out the sins I have committed, the wrongs I have done. I have felt the pangs of the Holy Spirit, Lord. I am now aware of the misstep I took. My heart is so heavy. Lift me up, Lord. Help me not to wallow in discouragement but to bask in Your forgiveness that is everlasting.

DAY 2
Immediate and Boundless Forgiveness

For I acknowledge my transgressions, and my sin is always before me.
Against You, You only, have I sinned, and done this evil in Your sight—
that You may be found just when You speak, and blameless when You judge.
PSALM 51:3–4 NKJV

*J*esus, no matter where I go, I cannot run from the sin I have committed. It is always right there in front of my face. So I now confess it to You. For it is You I have wronged. Rescue me, Lord, from this awful predicament. Help me to realize that Your forgiveness is not only boundless but immediate. Help me to put this wrongdoing behind me and move forward in Your will and way.

DAY 3
Honesty, the Blessed Policy

Behold, You desire truth in the inward parts,
and in the hidden part You will make me to know wisdom.
PSALM 51:6 NKJV

*L*ord, I can no longer lie to myself. I need to come to You in truth. My misdeed is weighing me down, Lord. I bring it now into Your light so that You can blast it away. Give me wisdom, Lord, to handle this situation better the next time. Your Word says that You will help the contrite and brokenhearted, Lord. Right now, that's me. So please, help me, heal me, make me whole.

Day 4
Habit in Hiding

Create in me a clean heart, O God, and renew a steadfast spirit within me.
Do not cast me away from Your presence, and do not take Your Holy Spirit from
me. Restore to me the joy of Your salvation, and uphold me by Your generous Spirit.
Psalm 51:10–12 NKJV

I feel like I've been wallowing in mud, Lord. I need to calmly yet boldly lift myself up and make a confession to You. I've got this habit that I've been hiding from others and supposedly from You. But who am I kidding? You know and see all. So Lord, I come to You today, seeking Your help. Work through me, Lord, to help me break this habit. Restore me to Your joy.

Day 5
Fly Like an Eagle

As far as the east is from the west, so far
has He removed our transgressions from us.
Psalm 103:12 NKJV

I cannot even fathom, Lord, how far away You remove our sins from us. But I still feel so guilty and discouraged. I want to get back up, walking in Your way. Yet my feet feel stuck. Lift me, Lord, up and out of this pit of despair. Help me to understand the fact that You've not only forgiven me of my sin but have forgotten all about it. Bring me back into Your saving grace.

DAY 6
God-Scan

Search me, O God, and know my heart: try me, and know my thoughts:
and see if there be any wicked way in me, and lead me in the way everlasting.
PSALM 139:23–24 KJV

I'm here for a God-scan, Lord. Please examine my body, mind, heart, and soul for anything that is displeasing to You. I don't want to fall into any temptations. So if there is anything You need me to hand over to You—and leave there—point it out to me. With You, the yoke is easy and the burden light. Thank You for saving me from shadows and bringing me into Your Son's Light.

DAY 7
Eyes on Jesus

Let us run with patience the race that
is set before us, looking unto Jesus.
HEBREWS 12:1–2 KJV

My eyes are off the mistakes I've made, the failures I've had. I am looking to You, Jesus, to help me through this life in You. I'm armed with Your patience—for I don't have any of my own. And with You holding my hand, running beside me, I can conquer any habit, any sin. Thank You, Lord, for never leaving me, for never running out on me. I praise Your name!

Chapter 12:
Challenges Seeing God's
Hand in Everything

Our days are in God's hands. He is all-sufficient to meet our needs,
and the Savior is with us every step of the way.
ELIZABETH GEORGE, *GOD'S GARDEN OF GRACE*

. . . .

*O*ne of the greatest challenges facing believers is discerning God's purpose and presence with us in the midst of our trials. Many people have confessed that although they can submit to things that come from God's hand, they have great difficulty submitting to other humans, through whom most of their troubles come. Or they give their hearts to trusting God, but then someone comes along whose actions threaten their endeavors. Although they may have no difficulty trusting God, they have serious issues with trusting their fellow man (or woman).

Almost everything we encounter in our lives comes to us through human instrumentalities, and most of our trials are the result of some man or woman's failure, ignorance, carelessness, cruelty, or sin. But how could an all-loving God put us through such heartbreak?

Hannah Whitall Smith wrote, "Moreover, things in which we can see God's hands always have a sweetness in them that comforts while it wounds. But the trials inflicted by man are full of nothing but bitterness." She continued:

> *What is needed, then, is to see God in everything and to receive everything*
> *directly from His hands with no intervention of second causes. And it is to this*
> *that we must be brought before we can know an abiding experience of entire*
> *abandonment and perfect trust. Our abandonment must be to God, not to*

man. And our trust must be in Him, not in any arm of flesh, or we shall fail at the first trial.

Let's turn to scripture to support Smith's claim that there are no "second causes" for the believing Christian—that everything comes to us through our Father's hand and with His knowledge, no matter what person or circumstances may have been the apparent agents.

- Not one sparrow falls to the ground without God knowing about it.
- He even knows how many hairs are on our head.
- We need not worry about our needs because the Father knows what we need.
- We need not seek revenge because God will do it for us.
- We need not fear because God is on our side.
- No one can stand against us because God is for us.
- Because we have God as our Shepherd, we are never in need.
- When we pass through the waters and the fire, God is with us.
- We are not harmed by lions because God shuts their mouths.
- We need not be concerned by what our fellow humans do to us because God is our Helper, and He will neither leave us nor forsake us. (See Psalm 23:1; Psalm 118:6; Isaiah 43:2; Daniel 6:22; Matthew 10:29–30; 6:32; Romans 12:19; Romans 8:31; Hebrews 13:5–6.)

Thus, second causes are under the management of our Father. Not one of them can reach us without God's permission and knowledge. Everything (except our own sinfulness) comes from our Lord. "It may be the sin of man that originates the action, and therefore the thing itself cannot be said to be the will of God," Smith wrote, "but by the time it reaches us, it has become God's will for us and must be accepted as coming directly from His hands."

And never forget that, through it all, God will be with you, laughing with you during times of joy and comforting you through times of trial. Imagine you are the man who has been beaten and robbed and is lying on the side of the road. Others may pass by, but you look up at the One who has paused by your side. It is the face of Jesus. He will put oil on your wounds, bind you up, pick you up, and carry you to a place of warmth and comfort, providing for you until you are back on your feet.

In all things we must be patient and totally abandoned to God's will and way, to His plan for us, through every blessing as well as every trial. For God loved Jesus as much on the cross as He did on Mount Tabor (where Jesus was transfigured).

We are like a child in God's arms. Everything that touches us goes through Him first. We must realize that no evil exists—no matter how dark and bleak—that God cannot turn into good.

Take the case of Joseph. Instead of killing him, his brothers sold him to some merchants. After serving as a slave, being accused of rape and thrown into a dungeon, Joseph became the number-two man in Egypt and was later able to save the lives of his father and his brothers and their families. He told his siblings, "Don't be sad or angry with yourselves that you sold me. . . . God sent me ahead of you to make sure that you would have descendants on the earth and to save your lives in an amazing way. It wasn't you who sent me here, but God. . . . Even though you planned evil against me, God planned good to come out of it" (Genesis 45:5, 7–8; 50:20 GW). Through all Joseph's trials and successes, our Father God was with Joseph—and Joseph stayed with Him. "While Joseph was in prison, the LORD [the great I AM] was with him. The LORD reached out to him with his unchanging love and gave him protection. . . . The LORD was with Joseph and made whatever he did successful" (Genesis 39:20–21, 23 GW). Because Joseph stayed close to the Lord, our Creator God turned Joseph's trial into a blessing—not only for Joseph himself but for the sons of Israel! And He promises to do the same for us!

God is not the author of sin, but He uses His creativity and His wisdom to work the design of His providence to His—and our—advantage. All we need to do is trust Him to work things out to our good. He will overrule events, trials, and tragedies in our lives to His glory!

Being women, we often try to fix things and get frustrated when we can't. Those are times when we need to let go and let God. Because *He* is the "Great Fixer."

Oftentimes, He sees solutions that we cannot even imagine! After all, He is the *Creator* God. As the great I AM, He has everything under His power. Are you allowing God to work in the events of your life—or are you too busy "fixing them" to let Him into the situations, thus blocking His way?

When our former pastor suddenly retired, the church's leaders not only had to scramble to keep the church going but had to begin the arduous process of interviewing potential replacements. At one point, we made an offer to one of the candidates, thinking he would be absolutely perfect for our small congregation. But it seemed to take him forever to accept our offer. After several weeks, he finally turned us down. We were devastated, wondering how—and when—God would answer our prayers. We asked Him, "Why, God? Why?"

So we began the interview process all over again, while also reconsidering former candidates. We finally made an offer to a new candidate and he accepted! We are thrilled with our new pastor—he is beyond what we ever could have hoped for or imagined! If the first candidate had accepted our offer, we would have missed out on the one who is a perfect fit! Because we were walking in God's will and in His way, trusting Him to come through for us, He created a wonderful solution, in *His* time. Granted—it took much patience and faith. But are these not the cornerstones of our belief?

When our dog Schaefer died, I ran around like a nut, trying to find a replacement for him. I made one bad choice after another. Finally, I let go and let God work in the situation. Today we have a shar-pei–yellow Lab mix, the best dog we've ever owned, who fills our lives with so much laughter! God turned our mourning into joy.

Like Dorothy in *The Wizard of Oz*, we sometimes have to go quite a distance down that long, yellow-brick road of loss, grief, tragedy, and trials before we find our way home. And the amazing thing about this is that many times we have incredible life-changing experiences and learn valuable lessons along the way.

Our God is an awesome God! He leads us through desert places. But if we keep our eyes on His pillar of light and follow the cloud He sends before us, we will have the living water we need to continue along the way. He will provide us with manna—His wonderful Word. He will continue to take care of us and will one day lead us to the

Promised Land (see Genesis 50:24–25).

Our part is to trust that everything we experience—good and bad—comes through Him to us. We are not to be beguiled by the darkness of doubts, what-ifs, and trials but to understand that He is with us in the midst of our storms and will find an awesomely creative way to turn whatever evil confronts us into our eventual good.

We need not enjoy our trials but simply understand that we must trust God's will, wisdom, and creativity in the midst of them and impress the certainty upon our minds that He is with us through it all until the end of the age (see Matthew 28:20). Knowing this, we can simply let go with abandon and let God work His marvels in good times and bad, praising Him all the way.

> *For by praising Him in and for your circumstance,*
> *you leave God two alternatives: Change the circumstance,*
> *or give you so much grace that you'll actually become*
> *glad for the experience. Either way, you're the winner.*
> BILL GILLHAM, *WHAT GOD WISHES CHRISTIANS KNEW ABOUT CHRISTIANITY*

$\mathcal{P}$ATH MARKERS

$\mathcal{P}$romise

We are assured and know that [God being a partner in their labor] all things
work together and are [fitting into a plan] for good to and for those who love God
and are called according to [His] design and purpose.

ROMANS 8:28 AMP

$\mathcal{P}$roof

[Nebuchadnezzar] commanded the most mighty men that were in his army to bind
Shadrach, Meshach, and Abednego, and to cast them into the burning fiery furnace.
Then these men were bound in their coats, their hosen, and their hats, and their other
garments, and were cast into the midst of the burning fiery furnace. . . .

Then Nebuchadnezzar the king was astonished, and rose up in haste, and
spake, and said unto his counsellors, Did not we cast three men bound into the
midst of the fire? They answered and said unto the king, True, O king.

He answered and said, Lo, I see four men loose, walking in the midst of
the fire, and they have no hurt; and the form of the fourth is like the Son of God.
Then Nebuchadnezzar came near to the mouth of the burning fiery furnace, and
spake, and said, Shadrach, Meshach, and Abednego, ye servants of the most high
God, come forth, and come hither. Then Shadrach, Meshach, and Abednego, came
forth of the midst of the fire. And the princes, governors, and captains, and the
king's counsellors, being gathered together, saw these men, upon whose bodies the
fire had no power, nor was an hair of their head singed, neither were their coats
changed, nor the smell of fire had passed on them.

Then Nebuchadnezzar spake, and said, Blessed be the God of Shadrach,
Meshach, and Abednego, who hath sent his angel, and delivered his servants that
trusted in him, and have changed the king's word, and yielded their bodies, that
they might not serve nor worship any god, except their own God.

DANIEL 3:20, 24–28 KJV

Provision

Blessed be the God and Father of our Lord Jesus Christ, the Father of sympathy (pity and mercy) and the God [Who is the Source] of every comfort (consolation and encouragement), Who comforts (consoles and encourages) us in every trouble (calamity and affliction), so that we may also be able to comfort (console and encourage) those who are in any kind of trouble or distress, with the comfort (consolation and encouragement) with which we ourselves are comforted (consoled and encouraged) by God.

2 CORINTHIANS 1:3–4 AMP

Portrait

I am assured of God's presence in any and all situations (see Isaiah 43:2).

MIND-RENEWING PRAYERS

DAY 1
God Reality

When you pass through the waters, I will be with you; and through the rivers, they shall not overflow you. When you walk through the fire, you shall not be burned, nor shall the flame scorch you.
ISAIAH 43:2 NKJV

Lord, I feel as if I am being tossed from floodwaters to the furnace and back again. But that's only how I feel—I know it is not reality. My reality is that You are here beside me—through fire and water. There is no need for me to freak out about anything. My comfort is that You are with me and that You will work all things out to my good. And in that fact I rest.

DAY 2
God's Grand Plan

The LORD is on my side; I will not fear.
What can man do to me?
PSALM 118:6 NKJV

I'm in a tough spot, God. I feel fear rising up within me. But I know You are on my side. And although it's hard for me to fathom how this will turn out, I know you have something up Your sleeve. I don't need to know the details. All I need is to look to You. To trust that in Your wisdom and creativity, You will work this into Your grand plan. That gives me courage and great peace.

DAY 3
From Panic to Praise

"Give your entire attention to what God is doing right now, and don't get
worked up about what may or may not happen tomorrow. God will help
you deal with whatever hard things come up when the time comes."
MATTHEW 6:34 MSG

The future is so uncertain, Lord. I find myself wishing my life away, just so I can get on the other side of this trial I am going through. A thousand different scenarios about what may or may not happen are ricocheting around in my head. Help me to find Your peace. Take my hand and lead me into Your light. Change my thoughts from panic to praise!

DAY 4
The Face of the Good Samaritan

They should seek the Lord, if haply they might feel after him,
and find him, though he be not far from every one of us:
for in him we live, and move, and have our being.
ACTS 17:27–28 KJV

*Y*ou are never far away from me, Lord. Thank You, God! You are in every facet of my being. I cannot take a step without You knowing, guiding, leading. You take such good care of me. I need never fret or moan or fear. In Your presence, I am in the best hands ever!

DAY 5
Flying Right

"What's the price of a pet canary? Some loose change, right? And God cares
what happens to it even more than you do. He pays even greater attention to you,
down to the last detail—even numbering the hairs on your head!"
MATTHEW 10:29–30 MSG

*S*ometimes I'm such a birdbrain. But even then, God, You love me. Without You, I could never fly right. You are in every facet of my life. You know me so well, I sometimes wonder why You put up with me. And then I remember—it's because You love me, even knowing every detail about me. I am humbled in Your presence. Thank You, Lord, for giving me such love.

DAY 6
Everlasting, Unchanging Love

While Joseph was in prison, the LORD was with him. The LORD reached
out to him with his unchanging love and gave him protection. . . .
The LORD was with Joseph and made whatever he did successful.
GENESIS 39:20–21, 23 GW

I feel so alone and unloved, Lord. But as I lie here, I am imagining You reaching out to me with everlasting love. I see You surrounding me with Your light. You are my rock, my refuge, my fortress. In You, nothing can ever harm me. With You, I have success, because You are working through me. To Your glory, Lord.

DAY 7
Praise, Praise, Praise!

We can rejoice, too, when we run into problems and trials, for we know that
they help us develop endurance. And endurance develops strength of character,
and character strengthens our confident hope of salvation.
ROMANS 5:3–4 NLT

I'm determined to rejoice in the midst of this trial, Lord. Through my tears and pain, I give You praise and sing Your name. In this life, Lord, I want to glorify You. You will give me the strength and courage to face anything—any man, woman, or child. Through You I can love them unconditionally and forgive any misdeeds. Praise, praise, praise!

Notes

PART 3:

Results

Chapter 13:
Slave Girl or Free Woman

*God is committed to freeing His children
from every lie, snare, and bondage.*
LISA BEVERE, *YOU ARE NOT WHAT YOU WEIGH*

....

Christian women have a choice. We can live in bondage or we can experience the freedom that life in Christ affords.

In the first scenario, the believer's soul is controlled by an unyielding obligation to obey the laws of God, either because she fears God will punish her or she expects some kind of remuneration for the duties she performs. In the second scenario, the controlling authority is a new *inner* woman who works out the will of the divine Creator without fear of being punished or for a reward. In the first, the Christian is a slave, walking in the flesh, hoping that her actions will please her overseer. In the second, she is free in Christ, a daughter of the King, an heir to His promises, walking in the Spirit, and working simply for love of her God.

The true pathway, of course, is that of the free woman and should be the route of all Christians. But sadly, once we have begun our initial walks, we are often led astray, falling back into our former lives of bondage to the world.

This misstep from freedom back into bondage occurred in the church in Galatia. In his letter to that congregation, the apostle Paul addressed the fact that some Jewish believers were insisting that Gentile believers obey the ceremonies and rites of Jewish law. On one occasion, even Peter and Barnabas had sided with these legalistic Jews (called Judaizers). Paul wrote:

Peter ate with the non-Jewish people until some Jewish people sent from James came to Antioch. When they arrived, Peter stopped eating with those who

weren't Jewish, and he separated himself from them. He was afraid of the Jews.
So Peter was a hypocrite, as were the other Jewish believers who joined with
him. Even Barnabas was influenced by what these Jewish believers did.

GALATIANS 2:12–13 NCV

Apparently, even the best of men (and women) can fall back into bondage by stumbling off the true path. In this case, Peter found himself reverting back to Jewish law and took Barnabas down with him. This was his attempt to please men instead of God. But Paul, who had confronted Peter, now set his readers straight, telling them, "We know that a person is made right with God not by following the law, but by trusting in Jesus Christ" (Galatians 2:16 NCV).

Thus, we are saved through our faith in Christ, and Christ alone. Anything we add to that formula is not of God and puts us in bondage. The Judaizers added ceremonial law. We add religious routines and our own egos (glorifying ourselves instead of God). Sometimes we add our Christian works, substituting them for faith. But make this clear in your mind: God is not so much interested in what you *do* as He is in what you *are*. God has His eye on your inner woman, the new creature born when you first accepted Christ.

In Galatians 4:24–31, Paul presents an analogy to help us understand that we are free women and not slaves. It's the story of Abraham, who had two sons, one by his wife, Sarah, and the other by her slave, Hagar. In Paul's analogy, Hagar represents the law while Sarah represents God's grace. Ishmael, Hagar's son, was born as a result of human conniving. Isaac, Sarah's son, was born as a result of God's good promise. As spiritually reborn children of God's promise, we freedwomen cannot go back to lives of slavery under the law! Remember, Ishmael was sent away once the promised son had arrived—because law and grace cannot exist together!

To help you understand the difference between the bondage of the law and the freedom-filled Gospel of Christ and to perhaps discover where your own bondage or freedom lies, here are a few comparisons:

The Law Says. . .	The Gospel Says. . .

"*Do* this and you will live."
(Luke 10:28 NASB)

"*Live* and then you will do."
(see Galatians 5:16–18)

"*Pay* me what you owe."
(Matthew 18:28 KJV)

"I *forgive* you everything."
(see 1 John 1:9)

"*Make* yourselves a new heart
and a new spirit!"
(Ezekiel 18:31 NASB)

"I will *give* you a new heart
and put a new spirit within you."
(Ezekiel 36:26 NASB)

"*You must love* the LORD your God
with all your heart, all your soul,
and all your strength."
(Deuteronomy 6:5 NLT)

"This is real love—not that we loved God,
but that *he loved us* and sent his Son as a
sacrifice to take away our sins."
(1 John 4:10 NLT)

"*Cursed* is everyone who does not
obey commands that are
written in God's Book of the Law."
(Galatians 3:10 NLT)

"*Blessed* are those whose
lawless deeds are forgiven, and whose
sins are covered."
(Romans 4:7 NKJV)

"The *wages* of sin is death."
(Romans 6:23 NKJV)

"The *gift* of God *is* eternal life in Christ
Jesus our Lord." (Romans 6:23 NKJV)

"You *must be* holy."
(Leviticus 20:26 NIrV)

"Christ's death has *made* you holy."
(Colossians 1:22 NIrV)

"Do these things."
(Numbers 15:13 NASB)

"Everything is done!"
(John 19:30 CEV)

The Law Says. . .	The Gospel Says. . .
"Blessings are the result of *obedience*." (see Deuteronomy 11:27)	"Obedience is the result of *blessings*." (see James 1:25)
"The *seventh day* is the" sabbath of rest (Leviticus 23:3 KJV)	"The *first day* of the week, we gathered." (Acts 20:7 NLT)
"If. . ."	"Therefore. . ."
"The Law. . .once restrained and held us captive." (Romans 7:6 AMP)	"Christ Jesus has set you free from the law." (Romans 8:2 NASB)

How exhausting to live in bondage! Thank God Christ came to save us from the law of Moses, for there was no way we could satisfy its demands. Instead, He gave us two new laws to replace all others: "Love the Lord your God with all your heart and with all your soul and with all your mind (intellect). This is the great (most important, principal) and first commandment. And a second is like it: You shall love your neighbor as [you do] yourself" (Matthew 22:37–39 AMP).

When we are living in accordance with the law, we become severed from Christ. We find ourselves "fallen away from grace (from God's gracious favor and unmerited blessing)" (Galatians 5:4 AMP). But, ladies, let us be very clear upon this point: we are no longer under the law of Moses but under the law of Christ—to love God and each other. As we obey this law in Christ, we find ourselves walking not in the flesh but in the Spirit, recipients of God's great grace and bearers of good fruit!

God's law told us where we were falling short (see Galatians 3:24–25). And although it served to bring us to Christ (see Galatians 3:24–25), it can never save us. Only Christ can do that.

It may not be law that you have added to Christ but a certain ritual you believe will please others. Or it may be some work of which you are very proud (thus glorifying your own ego). Smith wrote that "a religion of bondage always exalts self. It is what *I* do—*my* efforts, *my* wrestlings, *my* faithfulness." This idea of self-aggrandizement reminds me of a line in the song "Travesty," by the group Immortality, oddly enough: "I can't see myself in your eyes anymore." Ladies, we are in bondage if what we hope to see in the eyes of others is our own reflection. Better that we be freedwomen, looking to leave the reflection of Christ in the eyes of others. "A religion of liberty leaves nothing to glory in," Smith wrote. "It is all Christ, and what He does, and what He is, and how wonderfully He saves."

The secret to our freedom is to be as God sees us—as little children. "You are no longer slaves, but God's children; and since you are his children, he has made you also heirs" (Galatians 4:7 TNIV). Get God's view of you set in your mind. Walk as if you are a daughter of the King—because you are! "Unless you change and become like little children, you will never enter the kingdom of heaven" (Matthew 18:3 TNIV).

Children of good parents do not need to struggle to survive. They don't need to earn or carry around their own money, for their fathers and mothers provide for them. Parents feed, clothe, shelter, and love the heirs of their own little kingdom. In such a way, our spiritual Father cares for us. He not only provides everything we need but gives us blessings besides. We need not worry, stress, or strain about the future. We need not become desperate for riches other than the ones He provides in Christ. We need not try to please anyone except Him—not others, not ourselves—but only to serve Him with great love and affection. He is not a hard master (see Matthew 25:24 NLT) but an affectionate and a loving Father.

Because God has sacrificed His Son, as God's heirs we can "walk about in freedom" (Psalm 119:45 TNIV), unfettered by the opinions of others—*including ourselves*. We are God's willing servants, not slaves. And because He works in us "to will and to act in order to fulfill his good purpose" (Philippians 2:13 TNIV), all we need to do is accept Him as our Father, become as little children, and allow Him to take over our lives—to put Him in the driver's seat. And we must not try to grab for the steering wheel, because whenever we do, we're bound to swerve off our path.

If we keep in mind how God views us, we will bear the fruit of His Spirit—"love, joy, peace, patience, kindness, goodness, faithfulness, gentleness and self-control.

Against such things there is no law" (Galatians 5:22–23 TNIV).

The entire key to your Christian life is to become as a little child, living and walking by the Spirit (see Galatians 5:25) and "[not in your own strength] for it is God Who is all the while effectually at work in you [energizing and creating in you the power and desire], both to will and to work for His good pleasure and satisfaction and delight" (Philippians 2:13 AMP). What a precious Daddy God you have! As God's daughter of the promises, having put aside all self-effort and self-dependence, you will receive "the unending (boundless, fathomless, incalculable, and exhaustless) riches of Christ [wealth which no human being could have searched out]" (Ephesians 3:8 AMP).

With our adoring eyes upon our Father—not on ourselves, others, or material things—we can relax. So rest in Daddy God. Recognize that you are His child, a beautiful daughter and heir, a free woman, a new creature in Christ. Allow His Spirit to have His way. Sit back and leave the driving to Him. And let the fun—and joy—begin!

Don't fall into the trap of self-defeat. Let God untangle the web of lies you've believed about yourself and set you free to find who you are in Him—a daughter of the King, worthy because of His shed blood, forgiven by His grace, and strengthened by His strong hand.
LAURIE LOVEJOY HILLIARD AND SHARON LOVEJOY AUTRY,
HOLD YOU, MOMMY

$\mathscr{P}$ATH MARKERS

$\mathscr{P}$romise

A new heart will I give you and a new spirit will I put within you.

EZEKIEL 36:26 AMP

Proof

The love of Christ controls and urges and impels us, because we are of the opinion and conviction that [if] One died for all, then all died; and He died for all, so that all those who live might live no longer to and for themselves, but to and for Him Who died and was raised again for their sake. Consequently, from now on we estimate and regard no one from a [purely] human point of view [in terms of natural standards of value]. [No] even though we once did estimate Christ from a human viewpoint and as a man, yet now [we have such knowledge of Him that] we know Him no longer [in terms of the flesh]. Therefore if any person is [ingrafted] in Christ (the Messiah) he is a new creation (a new creature altogether); the old [previous moral and spiritual condition] has passed away. Behold, the fresh and new has come!

2 CORINTHIANS 5:14–17 AMP

Provision

It is God Who is all the while effectually at work in you [energizing and creating in you the power and desire], both to will and to work for His good pleasure and satisfaction and delight.

PHILIPPIANS 2:13 AMP

Portrait

In Christ, I am a free woman, a daughter of God, and an heir of His promises (see Galatians 4:7).

Day 1
My Main Focus

After starting your Christian lives in the Spirit, why are you now trying to become
perfect by your own human effort? Have you experienced so much for nothing?
Surely it was not in vain, was it? I ask you again, does God give you the Holy
Spirit and work miracles among you because you obey the law? Of course not!
It is because you believe the message you heard about Christ.
GALATIANS 3:3–5 NLT

$\mathcal{L}$ord, I feel like such a fool. I've been trying to become perfect by *doing* things. But the reality is that all I need to do is *be* Your daughter. Help me to live my life as Your servant—not as a slave to the law. You are to be my main focus—not the approval of others, not my pride. I want to walk in freedom and in Your Spirit. I want to live for You—and You alone!

Day 2
Privilege Granted

To me, though I am the very least of all the saints (God's consecrated people),
this grace (favor, privilege) was granted and graciously entrusted: to proclaim to
the Gentiles the unending (boundless, fathomless, incalculable, and exhaustless)
riches of Christ [wealth which no human being could have searched out].
EPHESIANS 3:8 AMP

$\mathcal{S}$ometimes it seems so unfathomable that You, Father God, would want me as Your daughter and heir, that You would think I am worthy of Your infinite riches. You amaze me, Lord. What grace (unmerited favor) You have entrusted to me! I am blessed in so many ways, just because I believe and have given myself over to Your Son. It is more than I ever asked or imagined.

DAY 3
Faith versus Feelings

*Live freely, animated and motivated by God's Spirit. Then you won't feed
the compulsions of selfishness. For there is a root of sinful self-interest in us
that is at odds with a free spirit, just as the free spirit is incompatible with
selfishness. These two ways of life are antithetical, so that you cannot live
at times one way and at times another way according to how you feel
on any given day. Why don't you choose to be led by the Spirit and so
escape the erratic compulsions of a law-dominated existence?*
GALATIANS 5:16–18 MSG

Father God, I am so wrapped up in works and my own self-interest that I have lost
my footing on Your pathway. My free spirit is snared in these earthly trappings. I know
my ego and my spirit are like oil and water– -they do not mix! So help me, Jesus, not to
live according to my feelings but according to my faith. Break those chains, Lord. I now
claim the freedom found only in You.

DAY 4
No Greater Blessing

*[Jesus] said, "I tell you the truth, unless you turn from your sins and become like
little children, you will never get into the Kingdom of Heaven."*
MATTHEW 18:3 NLT

Oh Father God, it's so nice not to have to be in control. I see You as my Father,
smiling at me, keeping a tight hold on my hand, leading me in the right direction. I
know that You will take care of everything I need and that You intend only good for
me—no matter what others may say or how things may appear. My spirit is one with
Yours. There is no greater blessing.

Day 5
A Core Meltdown

Love the Lord your God with all your heart and with all your
soul and with all your mind (intellect). This is the great
(most important, principal) and first commandment. And a second
is like it: You shall love your neighbor as [you do] yourself.
MATTHEW 22:37–39 AMP

I come to You today, Lord, with all the love in my heart. The core of my spirit melts in adoration of You. My mind is not on earthly things but on the one thing that will get me through this life, this day, this moment—love for my Father God. In these moments, as I bask in my love for You, I find I am made whole and overflowing with love for others and myself. What amazing love!

Day 6
True Love

This is real love—not that we loved God, but that he
loved us and sent his Son as a sacrifice to take away our sins.
1 JOHN 4:10 NLT

I cannot imagine the boundlessness of Your everlasting, unconditional love—the fact that You gave up Your precious Son for me even while I was still so far away from You. I am humbled that You would do that just so You could restore Your relationship with me. I feel Your arms around me, Lord, giving me the courage to be all You want me to be, in spirit and in love.

Day 7
Spring of Living Water

"I am the Alpha and the Omega, the Beginning and the End. To the thirsty I will give water without cost from the spring of the water of life. Those who are victorious will inherit all this, and I will be their God and they will be my children."
REVELATION 21:6–7 TNIV

*L*ord, You were here at the beginning and You will be here at the end. You knew me from before the world was formed and You loved me before I was born. My mind reels with this knowledge. In You, I will have victory. I want others to see Your reflection when they encounter me. May Your shining through me bring others to the spring of living water only You can supply.

Chapter 14:
Growth

Only you will ever limit what you are for God.
KAY ARTHUR, *BELOVED*

....

$\mathcal{D}$r. Frank Crane, minister and essayist, wrote, "Growth is the key word that unlocks the universe. Growth is God's plan." We are, in fact, "God's garden and vineyard and field under cultivation" (1 Corinthians 3:9 AMP). Thus, it is clear that God created us to grow—physically, mentally, emotionally, and spiritually. If we look at ourselves and the people around us, we can see that everyone is in a different stage of growth in a myriad of areas. In this journey through life, we are all working at becoming what we believe God has called us to be. And because we are still works in process, in the midst of growth, not one of us is perfect.

We can thus banish the grief, shame, self-doubt, and self-condemnation that come upon us after we make choices that lead us in the wrong direction. These missteps are merely part of our growth process. Thus, we should take care not to succumb to constant and consistent thoughts of our failings. For as Dr. Crane wrote, "There is no failure in my life. There is a lot of imperfection, but growth implies imperfection."

As we grow up in Christ, embarking on the pathway God has marked out for us, He intends for us not to stagnate like the Dead Sea but to flow ever on to the place He bids us, nestled deep in His grace. We are not to have our flow impeded by getting hung up on our faults and failings. Instead, we can simply perceive any growing pains resulting from our missteps and imperfections as blessings, because for us who have not yet arrived, it's all about the journey. As Robert Louis Stevenson wrote, "Little do ye know your own blessedness; for to travel hopefully is a better thing than to arrive, and the true success is to labour." Our joy is found in the process of our growth! And finding that joy, amid our imperfection and immaturity, is what it's all about!

Here we are not speaking of physical growth, because except for the skull and pelvis bones, which continue to grow throughout adulthood, our bodies eventually stop growing.[2] (Although our ears and noses seem to grow larger, it's just cartilage breaking down and gravity taking over. Let's move on.) We are speaking of spiritual growth.

Second Peter 3:18 tells us we are to "grow in grace (undeserved favor, spiritual strength) and recognition and knowledge and understanding of our Lord and Savior Jesus Christ (the Messiah) (AMP)." When we are first saved, we are infants in this new life in Christ. As such, we are given milk because we cannot yet handle the meat of the Word (see 1 Corinthians 3:1–3). But thank the Lord, we need not remain mere babes.

Earthly parents become alarmed and seek medical advice if their babies do not grow physically. So would God our Father be alarmed if we, His children, do not continue to grow spiritually. Yet many of us feel as if we can accomplish this growth in our own power. Perhaps we believe that if we try to do greater and greater things, we will reach the epitome of spirituality. Yet like the flowers and trees, we cannot *make* ourselves grow. That job has been left in the hands of our Father. We are mere plantings of the Lord—for His glory (see Isaiah 60:21; 61:3).

Can you just imagine an impatient child trying to increase his physical height? It is possible, of course, to have a limb-lengthening surgery.[3] That's where doctors break bones in the legs and insert spacers between the broken bones, allowing the physicians to widen the gaps—which the human body will eventually fill and repair—by turning the spacers. Not only is this procedure expensive, it is also very painful, and many who are not pleased with their height would not even consider taking such a drastic measure.

Yet do we not attempt to do something similar when we feel we have lost our passion for our faith? When we feel we have not gotten anywhere, that our lives have not improved one iota? Do we not stretch and strain to get back to the place from which we started? In this I-want-it-now culture, we feel discouraged if we aren't where we think we should be in our spiritual growth. So how do we remedy this situation?

What we need to do is stop trying to grow *into* grace but endeavor to grow *in* grace. Hanah Whitall Smith provides a wonderful analogy to help us understand this concept:

[Some Christians] are like a rosebush planted by a gardener in the hard, stony path with a view to its growing into the flower-bed, and which has of course dwindled and withered in consequence instead of flourishing and maturing.

She likens such Christians to the Hebrews in the wilderness. All the fighting and wandering they did there did not help them obtain one inch of God's Promised Land. To get possession of it, they needed to actually *enter* it. Once they did, they quickly began winning battles.

And we must do the same. In order to grow in grace, we have to plant ourselves in it, allowing our roots to go deep into this life hidden in Christ. Once we do, our spiritual growth will take off, and we will progress beyond our imagination.

But again, how do we accomplish such spiritual growth in grace? First, we need to understand what grace is. It is not just God's unmerited favor, a gift He freely gives, requiring no action on our part. It is also His boundless, divine love poured out in a multitude of ways. It's an abundant, unconditional love, almost beyond human comprehension. Think of the best mother you've ever known or the best husband or the best friend. Take all of their love and multiply it by infinity, and you may have scratched the surface of God's grace to us and love for us. The only thing we need to do to receive such grace is accept it from God's loving hand!

Thus, to grow in grace, our souls must be planted in the very heart of God's love. We must steep ourselves in grace and allow it to surround us. God has it in His plan that we grow in such a way. We are to "consider the lilies of the field and learn thoroughly how they grow; they neither toil nor spin. Yet I tell you, even Solomon in all his magnificence (excellence, dignity, and grace) was not arrayed like one of these" (Matthew 6:28–29 AMP). In other words, it's all about allowing God to be in control and trusting Him to grow us as He desires, continually being open to His promptings. Yet this is difficult for us who never seem to stop worrying about things past, present, and future. But the Word tells us not to fret about the necessities of life, that none of us by worrying and being anxious can add one inch to our stature (see Matthew 6:27). In fact, worrying and spinning our wheels, like frenzied and harried gerbils, actually impedes our growth, for it reveals our doubts that God will, as promised, take care of us, just as He takes care of His lilies. It signals to God, and others, that since we doubt His provision, we must take things into our own hands. But in doing so, we end up fighting or resisting or impeding God's work, instead of yielding to Him and allowing Him to grow us up into the woman He wants us to be.

This does not mean we are to remain idle in our spiritual growth. But it does mean we need to trust God. Take it as fact that He will give us the light, water, food, and clothes we need to live physically, and everything we need spiritually. Growth will come as we wait upon Him, then peaceably and obediently do as He asks.

To be like the lily, you must understand that you have not chosen Christ but He has chosen you. He says that He has "[planted you], that you might go and bear fruit and keep on bearing" (John 15:16 AMP). That is how we got into His grace in the first place! So He has planted us as He has the lily, which revels in and responds to God's sunshine, water, and soil. The lily grows naturally. There is no stretching or straining to get something it has already been given. There is no unwarranted and fruitless toiling involved at all!

We need to learn the lily's secret. Acknowledge that we are planted in grace and then let God—the divine husbandman—have His way with us. We are to put ourselves in the light of the Son of Righteousness, allowing the dew from heaven to quench our thirst. And just be pliable and yielding to what He would have us be!

If we expend effort trying to make ourselves grow spiritually, fussing and straining at every turn, our fruit will bear witness to our unnecessary toiling. We will be burned out—a common malady in church workers. We will wilt under stress. We will look for relief in all the wrong places instead of looking to God. Our eyes will be on our own selves or our self-dependence and self-effort.

Meanwhile, God is watching our futile efforts, shaking His head as we run around like chickens with our heads cut off. Ladies, why do we feel we must do it all on our own? Did we create the baby that grows within our womb? Did we, through some effort on our part, form its tiny fingernails, its crop of hair, its heart, lungs, and eyes? No! God did it all. The only effort we expended was to take care of our body while the baby grew within us. Then in God's timing (and with a bit of pushing on our part), the baby came forth and into our arms.

As God makes the baby grow without it even being aware that it is indeed growing, He has planted us to grow spiritually. And we are utterly helpless to do anything but allow Him to do so and not hinder His work within us. For when we hinder Him, we expend all our energy, grow exhausted, and suddenly find ourselves growing backward rather than forward. We would be wise to tap into the lily's secret and grow in God's way.

Of course, we are not actually lilies. We are human beings with a modicum of intelligence. We have a certain degree of power and personal responsibility. Yet that's just where our hindrance to God's work comes in. Smith wrote:

What the lily is by nature we must be by an intelligent and free surrender. To be one of the lilies means an interior abandonment of the rarest kind. It means that we are to be infinitely passive, and yet infinitely active also: passive as regards self and its workings, active as regards attention and response to God.

What we need to do is step aside and allow God to work while being attentive to what He whispers in our ears and how He wants us to respond. When we do, we will be blessed and become more intimate in our knowledge of Him. We will prosper, bringing forth fruit, "some an hundredfold, some sixtyfold, some thirtyfold" (Matthew 13:8 KJV). God says:

"I will love them freely. . . . I will be like the dew to Israel; he shall grow like the lily, and lengthen his roots like Lebanon. His branches shall spread; his beauty shall be like an olive tree, and his fragrance like Lebanon."

HOSEA 14:4–6 NKJV

"Blessed is the man who trusts in the LORD, and whose hope is the LORD. For he shall be like a tree planted by the waters, which spreads out its roots by the river, and will not fear when heat comes; but its leaf will be green, and will not be anxious in the year of drought, nor will cease from yielding fruit."

JEREMIAH 17:7–8 NKJV

So, ladies, know that whether or not you are conscious of it, God has made you to grow. It's a fact. If you find yourself straining once again to be your own gardener, seeding when you think it's needed and perhaps even pruning yourself, here's a simple way to refocus yourself.

BE A LILY

Be careful for nothing. Simply pray with thanksgiving
and let God's peace reign.

Expect to bear fruit regardless of the storms, wind,
and pelting rain.

Abide in the Vine, Jesus Christ. Open a vein and
let Him flow into your life.

Let God have His way in everything, understanding
that He will make all things right.

Interpose no barrier to His life-giving power working in you.

Look to Jesus, trusting Him to keep you safe in His
garden of grace and love.

Yield yourself up entirely to His control,
letting your response be "Yes, Lord, yes."

$\mathcal{P}$ATH MARKERS

$\mathcal{P}$romise

Blessed is the person who. . .delights in the teachings of the LORD and reflects on his teachings day and night. He is like a tree planted beside streams—a tree that produces fruit in season and whose leaves do not wither. He succeeds in everything he does.

PSALM 1:1–3 GW

Proof

What actually took place is this: I tried keeping rules and working my head off to please God, and it didn't work. So I quit being a "law man" so that I could be God's man. Christ's life showed me how, and enabled me to do it. I identified myself completely with him. Indeed, I have been crucified with Christ. My ego is no longer central. It is no longer important that I appear righteous before you or have your good opinion, and I am no longer driven to impress God. Christ lives in me. The life you see me living is not "mine," but it is lived by faith in the Son of God, who loved me and gave himself for me. I am not going to go back on that. Is it not clear to you that to go back to that old rule-keeping, peer-pleasing religion would be an abandonment of everything personal and free in my relationship with God? I refuse to do that, to repudiate God's grace. If a living relationship with God could come by rule-keeping, then Christ died unnecessarily.

GALATIANS 2:19–21 MSG

Provision

"Here's what I want you to do: Find a quiet, secluded place so you won't be tempted to role-play before God. Just be there as simply and honestly as you can manage. The focus will shift from you to God, and you will begin to sense his grace."

MATTHEW 6:6 MSG

Portrait

In Christ, I am growing in the grace and knowledge of the Lord (see 2 Peter 3:18).

Mind-Renewing Prayers

Day 1
Blessed by Grace

Blessed (happy, enviably fortunate, and spiritually prosperous—
possessing the happiness produced by the experience of God's favor and
especially conditioned by the revelation of His grace, regardless of their
outward conditions) are the pure in heart, for they shall see God!

MATTHEW 5:8 AMP

Lord, I find such joy in Your wonderful gift of grace. I know that what is happening around me is not as significant as what is going on *within* me. I am rooting myself—heart, body, soul, and mind—in Your soil of grace. I look only to You to meet all my needs. So doing gives me an abundance of peace I have never known before. Thank You, Lord, for Your amazing grace!

Day 2
An Unfathomable Gift

For the LORD God is our sun and our shield. He gives us grace and glory.
The LORD will withhold no good thing from those who do what is right.
PSALM 84:11 NLT

God, You are everything to me. Because of Your unfathomable gift of grace, I know that I can trust You to meet my every need. I feel Your love within and about me. I bask in the light that You provide me every day. Your living water quenches my thirst. The meat of Your Word nourishes my spirit. I revel in the wonder that is You.

DAY 3
Empowered by the Grace of God

*But the apostles stayed there a long time, preaching boldly about the
grace of the Lord. And the Lord proved their message was true by
giving them power to do miraculous signs and wonders.*
ACTS 14:3 NLT

When our lives are hidden in You, Christ, You work miracles. Through You, we are
empowered to do mighty deeds. It is amazing how You can use us to do things we never
thought possible before. So here I am, Lord. I am offering myself up to You and Your
working in, with, and through me. In You, I believe and am fearless.

DAY 4
Planted in Grace

*"We believe that we are all saved the same way,
by the undeserved grace of the Lord Jesus."*
ACTS 15:11 NLT

Jesus, I am humbled that You would give up Your life for me. All I can offer in
return is to allow You to live through me now. God has planted me in Your grace. In
You, I have the peace of knowing I am safe, that You will provide everything I need, that
I need not stretch or strain but simply allow You to grow me into the person You need.
Thank You, Jesus, for saving me.

DAY 5
Consider the Lilies

And God is able to make all grace abound toward you, that you, always having all sufficiency in all things, may have an abundance for every good work.
2 CORINTHIANS 9:8 NKJV

*E*very day I am becoming more and more of what You want me to be. When my emotions threaten to take control, I "consider the lilies," and Your peace immediately enters in. I am focusing on You, Jesus, knowing that's what I need to do. In You is where I crave to be. Because once I've experienced growth in grace, it becomes a magnificent obsession.

DAY 6
Glorious Strength

And He [Jesus] said to me, "My grace is sufficient for you, for My strength is made perfect in weakness." Therefore most gladly I will rather boast in my infirmities, that the power of Christ may rest upon me.
2 CORINTHIANS 12:9 NKJV

*L*ord, allowing You to live Your life through me is so wonderful. For whenever I am weak, Your glorious strength shines through. In this lily-life, there is no longer a barrier between You and me. Thank You, Lord, for all You have done, all You are doing, and all You will do in my life—to Your glory!

DAY 7
Flourishing in Grace

He who leans on, trusts in, and is confident in his riches shall fall,
but the [uncompromisingly] righteous shall flourish like a green bough.
PROVERBS 11:28 AMP

Father God, there have been times I worried about my finances. But living a life hidden with Your Son, I am putting those anxieties behind me and resting in You. I know the plans You have for me are for hope and a future. Thus, I will flourish as You would have me do. Thank You for loving me so. Thank You for always watching over me.

Chapter 15:
Service

What do we live for, if not to make
life less difficult for each other?
GEORGE ELIOT

....

When first entering this life of Christ, many of us are full of joy and enthusiasm, wanting to do some sort of service for our wonderful Lord, for we have learned the command of Jesus to be the "servant of all" (Mark 9:35 KJV). But as the days and years pass, we may begin to feel like what was once our delight in serving has become drudgery. When that happens, we have moved from the freedom we experienced as Christ's workers, with the "May I?" of love on our lips, to the frenzied activity of anxious slaves, with the "Must I?" of duty expressed through gritted teeth.

When we feel anxious, beleaguered, disdainful, exhausted, and tied up in knots about our Christian work, or when we have an impending desire to find our way out of serving others, we can be sure we have stepped off our pathway and embarked upon a route of bondage. We must immediately step back and look at our situation with the means of breaking through to receive the power that awaits women hidden in Christ.

The first bondage is flagging energy and will to do God's work. We feel as if we are no longer strong enough to accomplish what God has asked us to do. So we either do it begrudgingly or not at all. Yet the fact of the matter is that God has intended us to do what He wills, for He has written it upon our hearts and planted the seeds within our minds as part of His new covenant with us (see Hebrews 8:10). He is working within you and through you to make your work not a duty but a pleasure. And He gives us the energy to do it:

> *[Not in your own strength] for it is God Who is all the while effectually at work*
> *in you [energizing and creating in you the power and desire], both to will*
> *and to work for His good pleasure and satisfaction and delight.*

PHILIPPIANS 2:13 AMP

In fact, your strength is your biggest weakness because it can be a hindrance to what God wants to do through you (see 2 Corinthians 12:9). We have all seen a mother playing patty-cake with her infant, who at that age lacks hand-eye coordination and muscular strength. She picks up the baby's arms and claps his hands together, then pats them, rolls them, and opens up his arms for the grand finale. The baby does nothing but yield himself up to his mother's control, and Mom does it all. The yielding is the baby's part; the responsibility, the mother's. The child has neither skill nor capacity to do the motions to patty-cake. His utter weakness is his greatest strength, and it provides his greatest delight!

To break through this bondage of flagging energy and desire to do God's work, we must go to prayer. Ask God to help you to understand that He has given you the energy and desire to do what He has called you to do. Envision that He is filling you up with everything you need to do the job. Recognize that your strength is your biggest weakness. "Yield yourselves unto God, as those that are alive from the dead, and your members as instruments of righteousness unto God" (Romans 6:13 KJV).

The second form of bondage is thinking we are not good enough to be serving in a particular way. We can't believe that God has called us to join the worship team, serve on the church board, or head the committee for vacation Bible school. What we need to understand is that God has already gone before us and prepared the way for us (see John 10:3–4). The way to break through is to build up our God-confidence by nurturing our spirits in the Word. We must read His promises, His truths, and apply them to our hearts. "Every Scripture is God-breathed (given by His inspiration) and profitable for instruction. . .and discipline in obedience, [and] for training in righteousness (in holy living, in conformity to God's will in thought, purpose, and action)" (2 Timothy 3:16 AMP). By reading the Word of God daily, slowly, prayerfully, we will feed our minds and spirits with great truths that will build us into the women He wants us to be.

The third bondage of service is doing things to exult ourselves or with the expectation of receiving an external reward. With that kind of pressure, no wonder many Christian workers fall by the wayside. They are so anxious to do something well and right to impress people that they find themselves filled with worry. These kinds of efforts detract from Jesus. If you are exalting yourself, you have taken the glory from Christ.

The remedy is to get our eyes off ourselves and back on God. "And whatever you do, do it heartily, as to the Lord and not to men, knowing that from the Lord you will receive the reward of the inheritance; for you serve the Lord Christ" (Colossians 3:23–24 NKJV). We are to be not human pleasers but God pleasers. Forget self. Humility will empower you to go forward, knowing that everything you do is for the Lord—and no one else!

The fourth form of bondage is discouragement and despair. The outreach project that was your idea hasn't brought anyone new into the church. You are ready to step down from being on the committee, to throw in the towel, as they say. This attitude indicates a lack of trust in God.

The breakthrough of empowerment for discouragement is rolling every care off on the Lord. "Commit your way to the Lord [roll and repose each care of your load on Him]; trust (lean on, rely on, and be confident) also in Him and He will bring it to pass" (Psalm 37:5 AMP). Instead of giving up, lean harder on God. He will see you through! It's the evil one who is pointing out all your faults and feeding your misgivings. Pray and trust God to give you persistence as well as the courage and care you need.

To break through despair, cultivate joy within yourself. Recognize that God has a plan for your life, "plans to prosper you and not to harm you, plans to give you hope and a future" (Jeremiah 29:11 TNIV). Take joy in that promise! Thank God for all He has done in your life already—and what He plans to do in your future. When you do, you will be so renewed that you will not be able to help expressing God-cheer! For who knows what blessings await you when you persevere!

The sixth form of bondage is the feeling that we are doing too little or not enough. The remedy is understanding your responsibility in the matter. You are accountable for doing what God has called you to do and what He has given you the talents to perform—nothing more and nothing less. Remember that the work is God's, that He gives to each "according to his [or her] ability" (Matthew 25:15 TNIV). What a relief that the work is God's—and you are just His instrument! You are just the chisel in the hands of the great sculptor. That truth takes all the pressure off! We can rest in knowing that the Lord will tell us "the way in which we should walk and the thing that we should do" (Jeremiah 42:3 NASB), and we need not entertain what-if thoughts. So take on your responsibilities in God's strength, under His constant guidance, and by His leading. There is no need to be timid or worried. Just fill one sphere of responsibility, for one door opens to larger things, and another to still larger things, until you find yourself doing, in God's power, tasks you never believed or imagined you'd be doing (see Matthew 25:21). And in accordance with His timing, you'll be exactly where He wants you to be.

The seventh form of bondage concerns the reflections that always follow the completion of any endeavor. These particular afterthoughts come in two varieties. Either we congratulate ourselves upon the endeavor's success and are lifted up, or we are distressed over its failure and are utterly cast down. The breakthrough is to put the final results of any task in God's hands—and *leave them there*! "But this one thing I do, forgetting those things which are behind, and reaching forth unto those things which are before" (Philippians 3:13 KJV). Know that God is always pleased with your efforts and move on to the next thing. Refuse to worry. Simply ask God to override any mistakes and to bless your efforts as He chooses.

Through all your endeavors, be sure that God and His will are your motivating powers. Plug in to His Word to keep you fit and nourished, unfettered of stress, and free of worry. Continually seek His guidance and direction through prayer, then exercise your faith by taking bold steps where no woman has ever gone before—for God's glory and His glory alone. Know that He will never give you a task without giving you the strength, courage, and means to accomplish it. Leave the results with Him, and He will bless you and all your endeavors. When you do, may He say:

Well done, you upright (honorable, admirable)
and faithful servant! You have been faithful and trustworthy
over a little; I will put you in charge of much. Enter into and share
the joy (the delight, the blessedness) which your master enjoys.
MATTHEW 25:21 AMP

$\mathcal{P}$ATH MARKERS

$\mathcal{P}$romise

"For I know the plans that I have for you," declares the LORD, "plans for welfare and not for calamity to give you a future and a hope."

JEREMIAH 29:11 NASB

$\mathcal{P}$roof

Down the road a way in Joppa there was a disciple named Tabitha, "Gazelle" in our language. She was well-known for doing good and helping out. During the time Peter was in the area she became sick and died. Her friends prepared her body for burial and put her in a cool room.

Some of the disciples had heard that Peter was visiting in nearby Lydda and sent two men to ask if he would be so kind as to come over. Peter got right up and went with them. They took him into the room where Tabitha's body was laid out. Her old friends, most of them widows, were in the room mourning. They showed Peter pieces of clothing the Gazelle had made while she was with them. Peter put the widows all out of the room. He knelt and prayed. Then he spoke directly to the body: "Tabitha, get up."

She opened her eyes. When she saw Peter, she sat up. He took her hand and helped her up. Then he called in the believers and widows, and presented her to them alive.

ACTS 9:36–41 MSG

$\mathcal{P}$rovision

Keep on doing what you've done from the beginning. . . . Better yet, redouble your efforts. Be energetic in your life of salvation, reverent and sensitive before God. That energy is God's energy, an energy deep within you, God himself willing and working at what will give him the most pleasure.

PHILIPPIANS 2:12–13 MSG

Portrait

In Christ, I am strong enough to do whatever God calls me to do (see Philippians 4:13).

Mind-Renewing Prayers

Day 1
A Tent of Strength and Power

*But He said to me, My grace (My favor and loving-kindness and mercy)
is enough for you [sufficient against any danger and enables you to
bear the trouble manfully]; for My strength and power are made perfect
(fulfilled and completed) and show themselves most effective in [your]
weakness. Therefore, I will all the more gladly glory in my weaknesses
and infirmities, that the strength and power of Christ (the Messiah)
may rest (yes, may pitch a tent over and dwell) upon me!*
2 Corinthians 12:9 amp

Jesus, Your grace and love are overwhelming. You give me the strength to do all that You have called me to do. Your power shines through my weakness. I am envisioning Your strength and power resting over me like a tent. There is nothing I cannot do! This is a truth that I will emblazon on my heart, for it will give me peace and confidence as I do Your will to Your glory!

Day 2
Knowing the Shepherd's Voice

He calleth his own sheep by name, and leadeth them out.
And when he putteth forth his own sheep, he goeth before them,
and the sheep follow him: for they know his voice.
JOHN 10:3–4 KJV

*L*ord Jesus, I need never fear for You always go before me, blazing a trail for me to follow. I am getting to know Your voice very well. The more time I spend with You, the more familiar it becomes. Thank You for giving us the Holy Spirit. With Your strength, His guidance, and the Father's protection, I step into the unknown, sure that You will be with me all the way.

Day 3
Secret Blessings

When you give to the poor, don't let anyone know about it. Then your gift will be
given in secret. Your Father knows what is done in secret, and he will reward you.
MATTHEW 6:3–4 CEV

*S*erving You can be done in so many different ways, Lord. I love giving little secret blessings to those I encounter in my daily endeavors, knowing that You are interested in the little things as well as the big. So each day, Lord, point out to me whom You would like me to secretly serve. Whisper in my ear how You would like me to bless them. And thank You for the joy this brings!

Day 4
One Desire

Do what the LORD wants, and he will give you your heart's desire.
Let the LORD lead you and trust him to help.
PSALM 37:4–5 CEV

God, it is amazing how You work through me to do the things You want me to do.
I am awed at how the things You desire are the things I grow to desire. So lead me on,
Lord. I know that whatever You have waiting out there for me is what You want me to
do. And wherever You lead me is exactly where You want me to go!

Day 5
Seeking Guidance

As each has received a gift, use it to serve one another, as good stewards
of God's varied grace: whoever speaks, as one who speaks oracles of God;
whoever serves, as one who serves by the strength that God supplies—
in order that in everything God may be glorified through Jesus Christ.
1 PETER 4:10–11 ESV

I'm not sure what my gift is, Lord, but I want to serve You. So I seek Your guidance.
What do You want me to do? Whom do You want me to serve? Lead me to the path You
want me to take. Open the doors You want me to enter. I want to do Your will, in Your
way and in Your timing. Give me patience to wait for Your call and ears to hear Your
instructions.

Day 6
Your Time

*"Who knows whether you have not come to
the kingdom for such a time as this?"*
ESTHER 4:14 ESV

I need Your courage, Lord. Like Esther, I am really stepping out, taking a major leap of faith. Remind me that the success of all my works is in Your hands, not mine. So I give the actual work, the strength to accomplish it, and its results to You. And I take up the mantle of Your peace, power, and perseverance to achieve what You're leading me to do.

Day 7
The Ultimate Project Manager

*"Well done, good and faithful servant! You have been faithful with a few things;
I will put you in charge of many things. Come and share your master's happiness!"*
MATTHEW 25:21 TNIV

Thanks for the "Attagirl," Lord. It has been a long, sometimes tough road, but the deed has been done. I will not worry about the results but leave them up to You as I reach out for the next task You have for me. Working together with You, there's nothing that can't be accomplished! That's amazing! What joy You give me! Thank You, God. You're the ultimate project manager!

Chapter 16:
The Daily Walk and Talk

We are weaving for God the garment,
the only garment, they may ever see by Him.
AMY CARMICHAEL, *FROM SUNRISE LAND: LETTERS FROM JAPAN*

....

*W*e who have determined to live the higher life, a life hidden in Christ, should be as a result of that life a "peculiar people" (1 Peter 2:9 KJV)—not conformed to this world but transformed by the renewing of our minds (see Romans 12:2) each and every day!

Yet it seems many believers are so satisfied with lives conformed to the world that in almost every aspect, there seems to be no discernible difference between Christians and non-Christians. In fact, many believers are discouraged, depressed, anxious, gloomy, negative, frowning, self-indulgent, and armed with sharp tongues or bitter spirits. And although they may be respected Christian leaders or avid workers in the church, they seem to know nothing about the realities of the higher life in Christ. Or they may have discovered the blessings of walking as Christ walked but they only assume that mantle when they are with their minister or other Christians. When they get home, they become other persons entirely.

Although you may not be a professional preacher, your life, your words, and your behavior do demonstrate to others what you believe. If you call yourself a Christian, when others see you they should see Christ, for "clearly you are an epistle of Christ" (2 Corinthians 3:3 NKJV). Hannah Whitall Smith wrote, "The life hid with Christ in God is a hidden life, as to its source, but it must not be hidden as to its practical results."

Paxton Hood related a wonderful parable, "The Vocation of the Preacher," about how we may be the only Bible others ever read:

The good St. Francis of Assisi once stepped down into the cloisters of his monastery, and laying his hand on the shoulder of a young monk, "Brother," said he, "let us go down into the town and preach." So they went forth, the venerable father and the young man. And they walked along upon their way, conversing as they went. They wound their way down the principal streets, round the lowly alleys and lanes, and even to the outskirts of the town, and to the village beyond, till they found themselves back at the monastery again. Then said the young monk, "Father, when shall we begin to preach?" And the father looked kindly down upon his son and said, "My child, we have been preaching; we were preaching while we were walking. We have been seen— looked at; our behaviour has been remarked; and so we have delivered a morning's sermon. Ah! My son, it is of no use that we walk anywhere to preach unless we preach as we walk."

If we are to be Christians who walk the walk and talk the talk, we had best be hidden in Christ 24/7—not just in front of other believers and the minister, but at home, at work, everywhere we go, and in everything we do!

A good place to gear ourselves up for the day's duties is early in the morning, setting our minds on heavenly things, not things of this earth (see Colossians 3:2). Matthew 6:33 tells us to "seek first the kingdom of God and His righteousness" (NKJV). In his commentary on this verse, Matthew Henry writes, "Seek this first every day; let waking thoughts be of God. Let him that is the First, have the first." Before our feet hit the floor, then, we can determine to clothe ourselves in Christ and practice the presence of God.

Bishop John H. Vincent has told us what it means to practice God's presence:

1. To think of God as present—here and now.
2. To repeat the thought, again and again—"God is now here."
3. To practice by concentration of all the faculties of the soul the consciousness of His actual presence here and now, saying over and over again, "God is now here," putting emphasis on every word of the sentence, repeating again

and again, each time putting emphasis on one word, and thinking with concentrated attention, and resolving to believe that God is here now.

4. To ask God, now actually present, to give spiritual vision—the vision calm, intelligent, deliberate, that genuine faith—faith with the will in it—is sure to give.

5. To take for granted, as real faith must do, that what God promises God Himself will do; and then—

6. In cold blood, with intellectual concentration, by an act of willpower leave the entire matter with God—going about your work, business, study, recreation, travel—doing everything you attempt to do with the secret and unchallengeable conviction that all is well and He is near.

With Christ's mantle without, the Spirit's power within, and God's presence surrounding each of us here and now, we will be expressing our Lord and Savior to everyone we meet! We will find ourselves walking as Christ walked. We will be a peculiar people— empowered, loving, keeping no record of wrongs, returning good for evil, gentle, meek, kind, and yielding. We will not stand up for our own rights but will stand up for those of others, doing nothing for our glory but all for the glory of God. And we will be Christlike in private as well as in public, every hour of every day and not just on special occasions. We will not be plagued with anxieties or what-ifs, because we know that only today is ours. God has given it to us from His loving hand. He has taken back all our yesterdays, and all our tomorrows are still in His hands. We will live happily in the consciousness of here and now. William Osler advises us to "banish the future. Live only for the hour and its allotted work. Think not of the amount to be accomplished, the difficulties to be overcome, or the end to be attained, but set earnestly at the little task at your elbow, letting that be sufficient for the day." We will meet challenges bravely and persistently rise above obstacles without discouragement.

Remember the story of the farmer's mule? One day, the mule fell into a dry well. Believing he couldn't save the animal, the farmer directed his sons to bury the faithful beast of burden. But each time the boys threw a shovelful of dirt on top of the mule, he simply tramped on it. Soon enough dirt had come down so that the mule just walked out. That which was intended to bury him was the very means by which he was raised up and out of his trouble! May you be such a "mule," overcoming your obstacles and troubles instead of wallowing in an abyss of self-pity and discouragement.

David Hume has said that "he is happy whose circumstances suit his temper; but he is more excellent who can suit his temper to any circumstance." How true! Here we must reflect, asking ourselves if our good tempers remain, no matter what.

Perhaps some of you are not there yet, but after reading about this higher life, you have begun to hear God's voice whispering in your ear, "This is the way, walk in it" (Isaiah 30:21 NKJV). Perhaps you have begun to feel uneasy about certain aspects of your life, attitudes, or habits that are troubling your soul. Perhaps you know of someone who is so Christlike that you envy her expressions, attitude, and behavior, wanting to have what she has.

There is a wonderful lady in my church who I believe is the epitome of the Christian woman whose life is indeed hidden in Christ. She served for many years as a deacon, directs the adult choir, and is head of the church prayer chain. Her demeanor is gentle and meek, yet she is full of joy. When you speak to her, you can see the light of Christ shining through! She truly possesses that which we profess! When I asked her recently what her secret is, she was taken aback. She humbly explained that she was nothing extraordinary, yet I vehemently disagreed.

Shaking her head and smiling, she simply said that every moment of every day, she prays to the Lord. It is an ongoing conversation because, she said, "He is with me always." She also takes care "to listen to the thoughts in my mind. Those that are not from the Lord, I banish immediately. Other than that, I just follow my Lord's commandments—to love Him with all my heart, soul, mind, and strength, and to love others as I do myself."

At one point in our conversation, she admitted that sometimes she does get angry. Looking at her husband nodding, she gave a gentle laugh. (No one is perfect.) But for the most part, she is living the life hidden in Christ. Her face, demeanor, and very being are so filled with the light of Christ that you want to spend time in her presence, basking in the glow she gives off!

We who endeavor to live the higher life must not only walk the walk but talk the talk. Today there are so many ways through which thoughtless words can injure people. We can send messages via cell phone, Twitter, e-mail, and Facebook. The Internet lines of communication are the most dangerous because we can quickly write something and send it off without much forethought on our part. And when reading our message, the recipient can, in turn, misinterpret our words because she cannot see our face or hear any inflection in our voice. We would be wise to be sure that any words sent with these tools be ones of encouragement only. Any response other than that would best be taken up in a face-to-face encounter.

Many times it is better to be a woman of few words. Proverbs 17:28 tells us that "even fools are thought wise if they keep silent, and discerning if they hold their tongues" (TNIV).

Today's lives are full of anxiety and to-do lists. We seem to be twittering endless hours away, blogging about inanities, telling people how we're spending our days instead of actually living them. We seem compelled forward only to satisfy our obsession for material things that we end up clinging to instead of God. In our evenings, rather than open up a Bible, we turn to *American Idol* for entertainment, our eyes glazed over as we sit in our chairs, watching people ruthlessly compete for center stage. Meanwhile, Jesus' birthplace has become a massive war zone where one group threatens to annihilate another in the name of God.

A simple Christianity, where we seek truth, strive to serve others, and do God's will, is more important now than ever before. The only solution to the emptiness of our lives, the seemingly ever-present threat of terrorism, and the fruitlessness of living in a society that seeks only to have more and then more is a transparent Christianity where others look at us and see Christ alone.

Are you tired of trying to live up to the world's expectations? Are you ready for a radical spiritual transformation? You can do it! "With God, all things are possible" (Matthew 19:26 TNIV). Put everything you are and hope to be in the hands of the Father of lights, who has promised us "every good and perfect gift" (James 1:17 TNIV). And cultivate joy for, as Henry Drummond wrote, "Joy is as much a matter of cause and effect as pain. No one can get joy by merely asking for it. It is one of the ripest fruits of the Christian life, and, like all fruit, must be grown."

Move forward in the power of quietness, knowing that God surrounds you, Christ is within you, and the Holy Spirit guides you. Recognize that your energies should not be used exclusively to pursue worldly means but to seek first His kingdom, knowing that He will provide whatever you need.

You are enfolded in God's love and power. Nothing can harm you, so rest in His care. Leave with Him yesterday. He is guiding you today. He is crowding tomorrow full of blessings and opportunities—so you have only cause for peace and expectancy. Rejoice in His safety, for you are His precious child. Know that there is nothing to fear, for behind you is God's infinite power. In front of you are endless possibilities, and you are surrounded by opportunity. Peace and power are yours in Him.

With God with us on our journey through life, we need never be afraid. Through our trials, He will build us into a holy people. Our experiences will lead us to the revelation of His truths. Through His love, we will follow the yearning to serve others. Each unit of our day presents us with an opportunity to build up our Christian character, to strengthen our faith, and to love and praise our God, through whom all our wants, needs, and desires will be met. How wonderful to be abandoned to the guidance of our divine Master and fearlessly living our lives to His glory. The best part is that we need not do anything in our own power. He will provide all the strength and courage we need. Our part is merely to yield ourselves to Him, and His part is to work. He will never give us a command for which He has not equipped us with the power and strength to obey. He will never leave us nor forsake us. In fact, just the opposite, for He always goes before us each little step of the way.

Afresh I seek thee. Lead me—once more I pray—
Even should it be against my will, thy way.
Let me not feel thee foreign any hour,
Or shrink from thee as an estranged power.
Through doubt, through faith, through bliss, through stark dismay,
Through sunshine, wind, or snow, or fog, or shower,
Draw me to thee who art my only day.
GEORGE MACDONALD, *DIARY OF AN OLD SOUL*

$\mathcal{P}$ATH MARKERS

$\mathcal{P}$romise

Don't love the world's ways. Don't love the world's goods. Love of the world squeezes out love for the Father. Practically everything that goes on in the world— wanting your own way, wanting everything for yourself, wanting to appear important—has nothing to do with the Father. It just isolates you from him. The world and all its wanting, wanting, wanting is on the way out—but whoever does what God wants is set for eternity.

1 John 2:15–17 MSG

$\mathcal{P}$roof

If you only look at us, you might well miss the brightness. We carry this precious Message around in the unadorned clay pots of our ordinary lives. That's to prevent anyone from confusing God's incomparable power with us. As it is, there's not much chance of that. You know for yourselves that we're not much to look at. We've been surrounded and battered by troubles, but we're not demoralized; we're not sure what to do, but we know that God knows what to do; we've been spiritually terrorized, but God hasn't left our side; we've been thrown down, but we haven't broken. What they did to Jesus, they do to us—trial and torture, mockery and murder; what Jesus did among them, he does in us—he lives! . . . So we're not giving up. How could we! Even though on the outside it often looks like things are falling apart on us, on the inside, where God is making new life, not a day goes by without his unfolding grace. These hard times are small potatoes compared to the coming good times, the lavish celebration prepared for us. There's far more here than meets the eye. The things we see now are here today, gone tomorrow. But the things we can't see now will last forever.

2 Corinthians 4:7–10, 16–18 MSG

Provision

For we are God's handiwork, created in Christ Jesus to do good works, which God prepared in advance for us to do.

EPHESIANS 2:10 TNIV

Portrait

In Christ, I am spiritually transformed with energy, strength, and purpose every day (see Romans 12:1–2).

MIND-RENEWING PRAYERS

DAY 1
A Pledge of Faith

Light, space, zest—that's GOD! So, with him on my side I'm fearless, afraid of no one and nothing.
PSALM 27:1 MSG

Because of You, Lord, I know I need never be afraid of anyone or anything in this world. You are great, mighty, powerful, and it is to You—and not the things or people of this world—I pledge my undying faith. I refuse to be caught up in the competition for affluence, to worship the almighty dollar. Instead, I come to You, my Master, seated in the heavenlies.

Day 2
It's All in the Mind

We have the mind of Christ (the Messiah) and do hold
the thoughts (feelings and purposes) of His heart.
1 CORINTHIANS 2:16 AMP

This life in Christ is an awesome adventure. I praise God that You, Jesus, live in me. Your thoughts are becoming my thoughts. My will is lining up with Your will. Your desires are becoming mine more and more every day! Show me the path You want me to walk today. Show me whom You want me to bless today. I want to do what You have created me to do.

Day 3
The True Hidden Treasure

If we say we are his, we must follow the example of Christ.
1 JOHN 2:6 CEV

Lord, I have surrendered myself to You. I want to follow Your path, not that of the world. Make me humble, gentle, and honest. Help me to forgive others, to love all, to seek You first above all things. Give me the strength to be not like this world but like You. For You are the true treasure hidden within me, the source of all power as You work through me to reach all.

DAY 4
The New Life

Your old life is dead. Your new life, which is your real life—even though invisible to spectators—is with Christ in God. He is your life. When Christ (your real life, remember) shows up again on this earth, you'll show up, too—the real you, the glorious you. Meanwhile, be content with obscurity, like Christ.
COLOSSIANS 3:3–4 MSG

You are the only reality, Jesus. This world is just a shadow of things to come. I am content in seeking all that You are. Possess me, Jesus. Fill me with Your light and power so that I can do the things You are calling me to do—and be! You are my life, my love, my light. With You I am never stumbling around in darkness. You are always beside me, advising, loving, and guiding.

DAY 5
Practicing the Presence

Set your minds and keep them set on what is above (the higher things), not on the things that are on the earth.
COLOSSIANS 3:2 AMP

Lord, my mind-set is totally off today, and I haven't even gotten out of bed yet. So I will be still before You, practicing the presence of God. You are now here. I pray for Your spiritual vision. I reach out with faith that You will do what You have promised to do. I leave my life, my regrets, my work in Your hands, knowing You will provide all I need every moment of this day.

DAY 6
Rich in Forbearance

Be gentle and forbearing with one another and, if one has a difference
(a grievance or complaint) against another, readily pardoning each other;
even as the Lord has [freely] forgiven you, so must you also [forgive].
COLOSSIANS 3:13 AMP

God, You have forgiven me for so many things. It is quite humbling. If You, in Your infinite mercy, can pardon me, I surely can pardon the person who has wronged me. I leave the situation in Your hands, knowing You will give me peace and the forgiveness I need to extend. Help me keep no record of wrongs and to be rich in forbearance. For that is Your will, Your way.

DAY 7
Daily Spiritual Workout

Exercise daily in God—no spiritual flabbiness, please! Workouts in the
gymnasium are useful, but a disciplined life in God is far more so, making
you fit both today and forever. You can count on this. Take it to heart. This is why
we've thrown ourselves into this venture so totally. We're banking on the living
God, Savior of all men and women, especially believers.
1 TIMOTHY 4:7–8 MSG

I'm ready, Lord, to exercise in You. It's a workout I cannot neglect. I love You, and I love seeking Your advice, protection, comfort, peace, and strength every moment of every day. I envision You right beside me. I'm talking to You (mentally and physically) all the time. You help me discern Your voice from others. And it is You I am following—no one and nothing else!

Chapter 17:
The Joy of Obedience

When Christ is at the center of our lives, when His glory is our goal,
when we refuse to be intimidated by life's obstacles, and when we
live totally for Christ in obedience, we will find a joy that will
carry us through the darkest of valleys.
DR. MICHAEL YOUSSEF, "JOY THROUGH CHRIST"

....

*I*f you have been fortunate in this life, you have at one time or another had a friend, lover, sister, brother, or child whom you really and truly loved. Because of that love, you found yourself desiring to do anything and everything for him or her. No sacrifice was too big when it was for this special loved one. When you were separated from this person, you longed for him or her to return to you quickly, if possible. It was almost as if these two separate persons—you and the other—had become one in thought, word, and deed.

I encountered such a friend at my church. As soon as we met, we connected. We share many interests, including our love for God. Others remark upon our relationship, describing us as long-lost sisters joined at the hip. When my friend wants or needs something, I will do all in my power to get it for her. Our time together gives us both such joy! Hannah Whitall Smith describes such a bond like this:

> *A union of soul takes place, which makes all that belongs to one the property of*
> *the other. Separate interests and separate paths in life are no longer possible. . . .*
> *The reserve and distance suitable to mere friendship become fatal in love.*
> *Love gives all, and must have all in return. The wishes of one become binding*
> *obligations to the other, and the deepest desire of each heart is that it may know*
> *every secret wish or longing of the other in order that it may fly on the wings of*
> *the wind to gratify it.*

May we have this kind of loving relationship with Jesus! He has given us everything, and He asks for us to be wholly surrendered to Him in return. Might we have the same type of measureless devotion to Him that He displayed for us on the cross! But perhaps at Jesus' call for utter abandonment to Him, you shrink back. It seems too risky, too difficult, too scary for you to give Him all He asks. You see others going through this life without even acknowledging His presence, and they seem to be getting along just fine. So why must you surrender yourself to the *n*th degree to this Son of God called Jesus?

Although you do not yet know it, when you surrender yourself to Christ and obey Him in everything, you will be fulfilling your spiritual destiny. In wholly binding your life to Him, you will discover the reality of the Almighty God! You will be walking in light, not darkness. You will have such an intimate relationship with the Creator that He will tell you things that those who are further away from Him do not know! All we need to do is be totally obedient to Him, to the point where like the psalmist we will declare, "I delight to do thy will, O my God" (Psalm 40:8 KJV), or as Jesus said, "My food (nourishment) is to do the will (pleasure) of Him Who sent Me" (John 4:34 AMP).

This privilege of surrender is one that is not demanded by God. It is a matter of our choice, part of our free will. But not abandoning ourselves to Him will keep us from having the joy of the Lord, for Jesus has said, "Blessed (happy and to be envied) rather are those who hear the Word of God and obey and practice it!" (Luke 11:28 AMP). If we obey (or keep) His commands, we prove our love for Him. In return, Christ will not only love what we're doing but will show Himself to us! The Amplified Bible says it this way:

> *The person who has My commands and keeps them is the one who [really] loves Me; and whoever [really] loves Me will be loved by My Father, and I [too] will love him and will show (reveal, manifest) Myself to him. [I will let Myself be clearly seen by him and make Myself real to him.]*

JOHN 14:21

Jesus makes this offer of an intimate, loving relationship to all who will say yes to Him, but all do not accept His invitation. Other interests and loves (of others or self) are too precious for them to cast aside. The future of heaven is still available to them, but they will miss out on the unfathomable joy of this present moment!

How wonderful that He so desires us to rely on Him instead of ourselves! He has such joy in our response to Him as our true love! It is beyond our understanding. He is continually knocking on our door, hoping we will let Him in (see Revelation 3:20). And when we do, we will be like women who have built their house not upon the sand, but upon Jesus—the Rock of Ages. With Him as our foundation, obeying Him and His Word every moment of every day, we will be able to keep our heads in times of temptation or persecution. We will keep our comfort, hope, peace, and joy in the midst of distressing situations; and we will be kept spurred on by His amazing power! When we keep on obeying Him, He will keep us safe, strong, resilient, and happy all through our lives!

Psalm 119 is a powerful prayer that exalts God's Word and the author's passionate desire to obey it:

> *Blessed are those whose lives have integrity, those who follow the teachings of the* LORD.
> *Blessed are those who obey his written instructions. They wholeheartedly search for him. . . . I find joy in the way shown by your written instructions more than I find joy in all kinds of riches. I want to reflect on your guiding principles and study your ways.*
> *Your laws make me happy. I never forget your word. Be kind to me so that I may live and hold on to your word. Uncover my eyes so that I may see the miraculous things in your teachings.*

PSALM 119:1–2, 14–18 GW

The psalmist tells God how blessed and happy are those who are wholly devoted to Him and obey His Word. In fact, in the God's Word translation of Psalm 119, the word *joy* is used four times (see 119:14, 111, 162) and *happy* nine times (see 119:16, 24, 35, 47, 70, 77, 92, 143, 174). God's teachings and commands have kept the psalmist not only from misery but from disaster! Twelve times he tells his readers of the *new life* (119:25, 37, 40, 50, 88, 93, 107, 149, 154, 156, 159, 175) he has received through this wonderful relationship with and knowledge of God.

Throughout Psalm 119, the author never brandishes his own opinion but refers only to God and what He has told him. For the only chance the psalmist has at a new life is to obey what God says in His Word, whether he understands it or not.

Like a child at her father's knee, we merely obey God's commands because He says so. And not only are we instructed to obey God and His commands diligently, but we are to meditate on them. For if we do not bathe ourselves in the Word, we will perhaps be unclear as to what He wants us to do. And the more we look to God for answers, the more we will begin to see everything through His eyes 24/7 and keep ourselves from immediately looking to others, or ourselves, for direction.

Let us be clear. God has chosen many to receive His grace and love and follow Him. But He requests this of us:

You shall love the Lord your God out of and with your whole heart and out of and with all your soul (your life) and out of and with all your mind (with your faculty of thought and your moral understanding) and out of and with all your strength. This is the first and principal commandment. The second is like it and is this, You shall love your neighbor as yourself. There is no other commandment greater than these.

MARK 12:30–31 AMP

If only our desire to chase after Him would be as great as our desire for a new pair of shoes or a purse! If you do not yet have that desire, pray that God would grant you passion for His Word, understanding of His love, and a desire to follow Him with everything you are!

It would be well for us to keep in mind that as we follow God's Word and obey His commands, we must not be concerned about the outcome.

God's training is for now, not presently. His purpose is for this minute, not for something in the future. We have nothing to do with the afterwards of obedience; we get wrong when we think of the afterward. What men call

training and preparation, God calls the end. God's end is to enable me to see
that He can walk on the chaos of my life just now. If we have a further end in
view, we do not pay sufficient attention to the immediate present: if we realize
that obedience is the end, then each moment as it comes is precious.

OSWALD CHAMBERS, MY UTMOST FOR HIS HIGHEST

Would that we would be like Abraham. When God spoke, he "did not confer
with flesh and blood" (Galatians 1:16 AMP)—he did not consult his own feelings or
insights or those of others)—but he went where God told him to and did what God
told him to do (see Genesis 22). When God spoke, Abraham simply responded, "Here
I am" (Genesis 22:1 NKJV). He listened to God's request (to sacrifice his son Isaac) and
did as commanded. There was no debate. No argument. No questions. He simply went
because God said so. Abraham obeyed, surrendered his son, and God revealed a ram as
a substitute for Isaac's life. What joy Abraham's obedience wrought!

God's revelations, His insights, are revealed to us the moment we obey.

Abruptly Jesus broke into prayer: "Thank you, Father, Lord of heaven and
earth. You've concealed your ways from sophisticates and know-it-alls, but
spelled them out clearly to ordinary people. Yes, Father, that's the way you like
to work."

MATTHEW 11.25 MSG

May we, too, abruptly break into prayer when God speaks to us, ordinary people,
and through our obedience does extraordinary things, not just in our lives but in the
lives of others. We need not understand what He is doing or why, merely faithfully step
out in obedience. Instantly, the next door opens, the sea parts, or the ram appears.

In this loving relationship with Christ, God may at times be silent. This is a sign
of the intimacy we have with Him, like an old couple who sit quietly together at times,
comfortable in each other's silent presence. This may be a moment in which we must
patiently await His next message, content with remaining with Him and meditating
on His Word. For if we run ahead, uncertain of His will, we may miss the miracle He is

about to perform. "When He heard that he [Lazarus] was sick, He stayed two more days in the place where He was" (John 11:6 NKJV).

Your love and devotion to Him are all the Lord asks of you as a reward for all He has done for you. Let yourself go—your entire self—mind, body, soul, strength, talents, spirit, everything you are! Lay it all before Him. Open the lines of communication by praying and digging into His Word, bathing yourself in it each day. Ask Him to help you live out the day in His will, His way. Request His power and spiritual insight to guide you in every task, relationship, and situation—from what to wear to what you read. Consciously recognize His presence in everything, and you will be brimming over with joy in His process as you find yourself lovingly embraced by this tender God, reaping the blessings of hearing His will and keeping it!

> *"Obey the LORD your God. Follow him by obeying*
> *his demands, his commands, his laws,*
> *and his rules that are written in the teachings of Moses.*
> *If you do these things, you will be successful in*
> *all you do and wherever you go."*
> 1 KINGS 2:3 NCV

$\mathcal{P}$ATH MARKERS

Promise

"But this is what I commanded them, saying, 'Obey My voice, and I will be your God, and you shall be My people. And walk in all the ways that I have commanded you, that it may be well with you.'"

JEREMIAH 7:23 NKJV

Proof

During the forty days after his crucifixion, he [Jesus] appeared to the apostles from time to time, and he proved to them in many ways that he was actually alive. And he talked to them about the Kingdom of God.

Once when he was eating with them, he commanded them, "Do not leave Jerusalem until the Father sends you the gift he promised, as I told you before. John baptized with water, but in just a few days you will be baptized with the Holy Spirit." . . .

On the day of Pentecost all the believers were meeting together in one place. Suddenly, there was a sound from heaven like the roaring of a mighty windstorm, and it filled the house where they were sitting. Then, what looked like flames or tongues of fire appeared and settled on each of them. And everyone present was filled with the Holy Spirit and began speaking in other languages, as the Holy Spirit gave them this ability.

ACTS 1:3–5; 2:1–4 NLT

Provision

Continue to work out your salvation with fear and trembling. It is God who produces in you the desires and actions that please him.

PHILIPPIANS 2:12–13 GW

Portrait

In Christ, I am loved by God and delight to do His will (see John 14:21).

MIND-RENEWING PRAYERS

DAY 1
A Glorious Mission

And we know that all things work together for good to those who
love God, to those who are the called according to His purpose.
ROMANS 8:28 NKJV

I love You so much, Lord, and although I don't always understand what is
happening, I know You will work everything out. All I need to do is stay focused on You
and obey all Your commands. For I am here to love You with all my heart, mind, body,
soul, and strength and to love others as myself. Serving You is a glorious mission. I
want no other master!

DAY 2
No Questions Asked

As a young man marries a young woman, so will your Builder marry you;
as a bridegroom rejoices over his bride, so will your God rejoice over you.
ISAIAH 62:5 TNIV

Lord, You are building me up to be the woman You want me to be. And You are as
happy with me as a bridegroom is with his bride. That's amazing! I feel so loved. Our
eternal relationship is something I can hardly grasp. But I can't help but smile. I feel
so valued—from my veil to my bridal slippers. Take my hand, Lord. Lead me on. I am
ready to follow You, no questions asked.

Day 3
Eager to Obey

"And all these blessings shall come upon you and overtake you,
because you obey the voice of the Lord your God."
DEUTERONOMY 28:2 NKJV

*W*ow! Being overtaken by blessings is a mind-boggling image. To imagine that
You are already working on my future blessings before I've even said, "Here I am, Lord!
Ready, willing, and able to do as You ask!" What a concept! Your promises make me
so eager to obey. So I come to You today, Lord, to await Your orders. My heart is wholly
dedicated to Your desires.

Day 4
Patiently Waiting

If you [really] love Me, you will keep (obey) My commands. And I will ask the
Father, and He will give you another Comforter (Counselor, Helper, Intercessor,
Advocate, Strengthener, and Standby), that He may remain with you forever.
JOHN 14:15–16 AMP

I need the Holy Spirit to speak to me, Lord. I am not sure what to do. I need advice.
I need the wisdom and strength that He can give me. Your Word says that You hear me
when I cry, when I call to You. I'm facing a situation in which I need Your courage.
If You remain silent, I'll take that as a signal to wait upon You. Help me not to rush
ahead but be patient, for I trust in You.

Day 5
Intimate with God

By faith, Noah built a ship in the middle of dry land. He was warned
about something he couldn't see, and acted on what he was told.
The result? His family was saved. His act of faith drew a sharp line between
the evil of the unbelieving world and the rightness of the believing world.
As a result, Noah became intimate with God.
HEBREWS 11:7 MSG

To have the faith of Noah, to build a huge ark in the desert, to ignore the heckling of worldlings as he goes out on a limb in obedience to You—that's the courage I'd like to have. For when we step out in faith, obeying everything You ask us to do, You work miracles, saving more than just us but also others in our lives. I want to be that intimate with You, Lord. Pull me close. I will obey.

Day 6
Digging Deep

Oh, how I love your law! I meditate on it all day long. Your commands
are always with me and make me wiser than my enemies. I have more
insight than all my teachers, for I meditate on your statutes. I have
more understanding than the elders, for I obey your precepts.
PSALM 119:97–100 TNIV

The more I get into Your Word, Lord, the closer I get to You. I am beginning to see things from Your perspective. This world is just a shadow to the light I see in You. I am digging deep, God, wanting to know all about You. I am letting Your Word linger in my mouth. It is the sweetest thing I know. Guide me on the path You want me to travel. I'm packed and ready to go!

DAY 7
God's Language of Love

*Your written instructions are miraculous. That is why I obey them. Your word
is a doorway that lets in light, and it helps gullible people understand.
I open my mouth and pant because I long for your commandments.*
PSALM 119:129–131 GW

I love opening Your Word, Lord. It takes me to new places. Even though I may
have read the same lines before, You prepare my heart beforehand to grasp their deeper
meaning. Your wisdom continually amazes me. I long to linger in Your language
of love. You are opening doorways to a new life, a new way, a new me. Continue to
enlighten me, Lord, as I make my way.

Chapter 18:
Divine Union

Hold on to Christ with your teeth
if your hands get crippled.
ELIZABETH PRENTISS, *MORE LOVE TO THEE:*
THE LIFE AND LETTERS OF ELIZABETH PRENTISS

· ·

Growing up, we read fairy tales about beautiful princesses who met or were rescued by princes. They fell in love and lived happily ever after. Later, if we married, we found that although we loved our spouses, they were far from the ideal prince. And if we will be honest with ourselves, we were far from being princesses.

Yet when we become Christians, we have a chance of actually fulfilling the happily-ever-after fairy tale with the one and only true Prince—Jesus Christ. He is the One who can rescue us from the poverty of ashes and the tower of temptation. With His kiss, we are awakened to a new reality. On Him alone can we rely, for He will never leave us. He is our comfort, peace, and rock. He is the One with whom we want to become one and live happily ever after.

God's entire plan for us "before the foundation of the world" (1 Peter 1:20 NASB) was for our souls and spirits to be united with our ultimate Bridegroom. This divine union is what Jesus prayed for—and not just for His disciples but for us, those who would later come to believe in Him. "That they all may be one, as You, Father, are in Me, and I in You; that they also may be one in Us, that the world may believe that You sent Me" (John 17:21 NKJV). This union was the "mystery which has been hidden from ages and from generations, but now has been revealed" (Colossians 1:26 NKJV). Because of Christ's death, we are right with God and can be united with Him (see Romans 6:4). It has been disclosed through the scriptures and "is made known to all nations" (Romans 16:26 AMP).

God has not made our union with Him difficult, nor has He kept it a secret. Yet some of us may not yet completely grasp the concept of being fully one with God. Perhaps our hearts do not fully believe it is available to us. Or we may be afraid to trust Him totally. Yet that is where this entire pathway of Christian life is leading to— *voluntarily* embracing a full oneness with God. He will not be satisfied until our spirits and souls have reached their destiny of a total and divine union with Him. "He shall see [the fruit] of the travail of His soul and be satisfied; by His knowledge of Himself [which He possesses and imparts to others] shall My [uncompromisingly] righteous One, My Servant, justify many and make many righteous" (Isaiah 53:11 AMP).

The usual path of Christian experience mirrors that of the first disciples. Jesus called them, awakening them to their need of Him. They looked up and immediately left their old lives to follow Him. Hearing His message, they believed. They worked for Him, talked with Him, walked with Him. But they were still so different from Him. They argued about who would be the greatest. Many times, they misunderstood His messages. At the end, all but one of them ran from the cross. Jesus still had sent them out to spread His message with their words and actions, empowering them to heal the sick— physically, emotionally, mentally, and spiritually. After His death, they cowered together in a locked room, wondering how they would survive the coming days. These disciples had known only the physical Christ as someone apart from them, their Teacher and Master, separate from them.

Then while they were in that upper room in Jerusalem, "without warning there was a sound like a strong wind, gale force—no one could tell where it came from. It filled the whole building. Then, like a wildfire, the Holy Spirit spread through their ranks" (Acts 2:2–4 MSG)! It was then—without warning—that the disciples were filled with Christ! There was no parting from Him now! They were one with Christ, filled with and aware of His life, spirit, and power within them.

Perhaps you have traveled this same path. You believe that Christ existed. That He was the Father's answer to our final reconciliation with Him. You have confidence that He loves you, that He is beside you and will walk with you through storm and fire, yet you have not given your complete heart, mind, body, and soul to Him but are holding back. Perhaps your will and His are not yet fully enjoined. Hannah Whitall Smith wrote:

You have not yet lost your own life that you may live only in His. Once it was "I and not Christ." Next it was "I and Christ." Perhaps now it is even "Christ and I." But has it come yet to be Christ only, and not I at all?

This miraculous union of our hearts and Christ's has been planned since the beginning of time and is meant for all of us. In fact, it happened when you accepted Christ. First Corinthians 3:16 tells us: "You realize, don't you, that you are the temple of God, and God himself is present in you? No one will get by with vandalizing God's temple, you can be sure of that. God's temple is sacred—and you, remember, are the temple" (MSG). Dwelling within you, a true believer, is the spirit of Christ. You are a temple of the living God. And if you read to whom this applies, you'll see that this scripture pertains to "mere infants [in the new life] in Christ" (1 Corinthians 3:1 AMP) who are still being fed with milk! So this is not a new dimension to your life as a believer. Christ has been residing in you all along! This is true of every Christian! You have already been transformed into a new creature!

The thing is that some may not yet have tuned into this fact or accepted it as a spiritual reality. They are not living in the full power imparted in this divine blending but are living as though it were not true. But as soon as you accept it as a reality through spirit, soul, and mind and devise to give up self, the power of oneness with God manifests itself to its *fullest* extent.

When we consciously and consistently recognize Christ within, the evidence of this union comes through in our character. For when we are truly, fully, and intimately one with Christ—allowing Him to have complete and utter reign over us—we are Christlike, for "anyone who claims to be intimate with God ought to live the same kind of life Jesus lived" (1 John 2:6 MSG). That means walking the walk and talking the talk. It means giving Christ not partial but full reign: "You are living the life of the Spirit, if the [Holy] Spirit of God [really] dwells within you [directs and controls you]" (Romans 8:9 AMP). It means being spent in love for others as Christ spent Himself in love for us (see John 21:17). Christ within impels us to feed His sheep, for He has told us, "As my Father hath sent me, even so send I you" (John 20:21 KJV).

Jesus said that "every tree is known by its own fruit" (Luke 6:44 NKJV). Those living in the full power of a union with Christ have natures that are loving, joyful, peaceful, longsuffering, kind, good, faithful, gentle, and self-controlled (see Galatians 5:22–23). Because you are fully aware that He is living through you, you won't be able to be anything but, for you have become "partakers of the divine nature" (2 Peter 1:4 NASB). Because He is holy, you will be holy. The godliness in you, full of light, will shine right through you and into the lives of others!

And it's not only our character that reveals we have become united with Christ. The things we do will also be a testament to the truth of our divine union. Jesus Himself said, "The Son cannot do anything on his own. He can do only what he sees the Father doing. Indeed, the Son does exactly what the Father does. . . . If I'm doing those things and you refuse to believe me, then at least believe the things that I'm doing. Then you will know and recognize that the Father is in me and that I am in the Father" (John 5:19; 10:38 GW).

This truth will be evident regardless of your emotions on a certain day. Smith says:

> *Pay no regard to your feelings, therefore, in this oneness with Christ, but see to it that you have the really vital fruits of a oneness in character and walk and mind. Your emotions may be very delightful, or they may be very depressing. In neither case are they any real indications of your spiritual state. . . .*
>
> *Your joy in the Lord is to be a far deeper thing than a mere emotion. It is to be the joy of knowledge, of perception, of actual existence.*

How wonderful to have a joy that is not tied to what happens to us throughout our days. Knowing that Christ is loving us within and sheltering us without, that no one can truly harm us, is contentment at its best.

It's also wonderful that our God never forces Himself upon us. Instead, He wants us to come to Him willingly. We are already God's living temple. Christ already resides in us, and we already received the Holy Spirit when we accepted Christ. What we need to do is continually, consistently, and completely *recognize* Christ's presence within us and *surrender* ourselves to Him.

Although you have known that Christ is in you, at times you may have ignored His presence, either through fear or disinterestedness or simply because you were too caught up in the things of this world. Perhaps there have been times you felt unprepared for Him, or perhaps you did not want Him to see the real you, so to save yourself embarrassment, you've kept Him at bay. While you have left Him waiting, you have missed out on the full peace, power, protection, guidance, insights, and other valuable treasures He could have bestowed upon you and into your life! Be at peace. He's patiently, lovingly waiting for you to look His way. He has already seen all that you are and all that you do—and loves you unconditionally.

So do not fear. Christ has been with you all along. He is ready to help you rest in Him. Allow Him to carry all your burdens, give you insights that only He would have, and empower you to live your life to the fullest 24/7. This is what you have been created for. For it is not you who lives, but Christ lives in you.

Because our partaking of the divine nature is not forced upon us but is something we volunteer to do, we must give our Prince a willing yes every minute of every day or the joy of our full and wonderful union with Him will be left wanting. In doing so, we need to acknowledge our oneness with Christ—it's a real thing. In addition, we need to lay down our wills, wholly surrendering ourselves—mind, body, spirit, and soul—to the Lord. We need to allow Him to take total possession of us and, in doing so, firmly believe that He has, indeed, taken possession of and is dwelling within us.

It is no longer we who live, but Christ who is living in us. Thus, we rely on and trust Him completely. All day and night, we steadfastly maintain this attitude, each knowing for certain this truth: "I have been crucified with Christ; it is no longer I who live, but Christ lives in me" (Galatians 2:20 NKJV). And what a life with Him we will have! By surrendering all to Him, we will possess nothing—and thereby everything! For He is all we truly need. Fully recognizing, acknowledging, and enjoying our union with Christ, we and our Prince can live together happily ever after!

For a child is born to us, a son is given to us.
The government will rest on his shoulders.
And he will be called: Wonderful Counselor, Mighty God,
Everlasting Father, Prince of Peace.
ISAIAH 9:6 NLT

𝒫ath Markers

𝒫romise

But whoever obeys what Christ says is the kind of person in whom God's love is perfected. That's how we know we are in Christ. Those who say that they live in him must live the same way he lived.

1 John 2:5–6 GW

𝒫roof

[Jesus prayed,] I tell you, if anyone steadfastly believes in Me, he will himself be able to do the things that I do; and he will do even greater things than these, because I go to the Father. . . .

I pray [it is not for their sake only that I make this request], but also for all those who will ever come to believe in (trust in, cling to, rely on) Me through their word and teaching, that they all may be one, [just] as You, Father, are in Me and I in You, that they also may be one in Us, so that the world may believe and be convinced that You have sent Me. . . .

Now as Peter went here and there among them all, he went down also to the saints who lived at Lydda. There he found a man named Aeneas, who had been bedfast for eight years and was paralyzed. And Peter said to him, Aeneas, Jesus Christ (the Messiah) [now] makes you whole. Get up and make your bed! And immediately [Aeneas] stood up. Then all the inhabitants of Lydda and the plain of Sharon saw [what had happened to] him and they turned to the Lord.

John 14:12; 17:20–21; Acts 9:32–35 AMP

𝒫rovision

Through his glory and integrity he has given us his promises that are of the highest value. Through these promises you will share in the divine nature because you have escaped the corruption that sinful desires cause in the world.

2 Peter 1:4 GW

Portrait

In Christ, I am spiritually blessed because He lives in me (see Ephesians 1:3).

Mind-Renewing Prayers

Day 1
Wonder-Filled Love

God chose him as your ransom long before the world began,
but he has now revealed him to you in these last days.
1 Peter 1:20 NLT

Lord, it is amazing that You planned the sacrifice of Your Son before the world had even begun. And all so that I could be reunited with You and Him! I have never known such wonder-filled love. I believe in the truth of Your Word, Lord. Show me, guide me through the scriptures. Speak to me through Your Word.

Day 2
Partaking of the Divine Nature

You surely know that your body is a temple where the Holy Spirit lives.
The Spirit is in you and is a gift from God. You are no longer your own.
1 Corinthians 6:19 CEV

I want to partake of Your divine nature, God. So I come to You, surrendering all that I am. I know Your Holy Spirit is within me, a gift from You. So I now give You a gift in return—*all* my heart, mind, body, and soul. Take possession of me, Lord. I am opening the door to You. Shine Your light throughout my being. Warm me with Your love. Illuminate me!

DAY 3
Divine Union

I have died, but Christ lives in me. And I now live by faith
in the Son of God, who loved me and gave his life for me.
GALATIANS 2:20 CEV

It is no longer I who live, Christ, but You are abiding within me. I am writing this upon my heart, Lord, and repeating it within my mind, for I desire this divine union. You are the prince of my life, and I give You my hand. I do! I am now living by faith that You have taken total possession of me and You are the true life within. Thank You for Your love, power, and sacrifice.

DAY 4
A Cornucopia of Love

The spiritual nature produces love, joy, peace, patience,
kindness, goodness, faithfulness, gentleness, and self-control.
GALATIANS 5:22–23 GW

Your life within me is shining its light into my world. May all who see me really see You through my character and my works. Thank You, Lord, for this overwhelming sense of peace, love, and joy. Thank You for all the fruit You are bearing in my life. I long for a full crop—an abundance of You within me, reaching out. A cornucopia of love within and without!

Day 5
Rising Above

*Put on the new self, which in the likeness of God has
been created in righteousness and holiness of the truth.*
EPHESIANS 4:24 NASB

*E*ach day, Lord, I remember that it is You living within me. Each hour I surrender myself to Your leading and love. Each moment I sense Your power to rise above this world. The true reality is our divine blending. May I rest in the peace that You are always with me, working through me, loving me—a new world without end, amen.

Day 6
Leaning Back

*But whoever obeys what Christ says is the kind of person in whom
God's love is perfected. That's how we know we are in Christ.*
1 JOHN 2:5 GW

*L*ord, I know I am not to believe my feelings. I am not to use them as a barometer of my life hidden with You. But I need Your help today. Let me rest in Your arms. Allow me to just lean back and let You take over. Show me the true way, the true life—that You and I are one, the perfect union. Keep me focused on You and Your love.

Day 7
A Taste of Heaven

All praise to God, the Father of our Lord Jesus Christ, who has blessed us with every spiritual blessing in the heavenly realms because we are united with Christ.
EPHESIANS 1:3 NLT

This divine union with You is a taste of heaven on earth. My prayer is not for anything but You. A oneness with Christ is my sole desire. With His presence within me, I know I am safe, blessed, loved, and empowered to be all that He wants me to be. Give me the passion, Lord, to extend Your love to others—no matter how I feel. For You are my truth, light, and way.

Chapter 19:
The Chariots of God

*Everything God teaches us about Himself is something that will
guide us through the trials of our lives. Everything He reveals
to us stretches our minds so that we can apply His
faithfulness everywhere we need it.*

KARON PHILLIPS GOODMAN, *YOU STILL HERE, LORD?*

....

*H*arriet Beecher Stowe once said that "earthly cares are a heavenly discipline."
Hannah Whitall Smith declared that "they are even something better than discipline—
they are God's chariots, sent to take the soul to its high places of triumph."

But often our earthly woes don't at all resemble God's chariots. Instead,
they manifest themselves as stresses, heartaches, disputes, trials, offenses,
misunderstandings, losses, and callousness. They are like juggernauts[4], steamrollers
that wound and crush our spirits, poised to roll right over us and sink us down into the
earth. But if, like Elisha, we could see these woes as God's vehicles of victory, we would
rise above these cares in triumph, attaining heights we never dreamed possible! The
juggernaut is the tangible, visible, earthly conveyance, whereas the chariot of God is the
intangible, invisible vehicle that will take us to the heavenly places.

To better understand the concept of the chariots of God, we need to delve into the
story found in 2 Kings 6. The king of Syria kept coming against Israel, but Elisha always
knew via supernatural revelation exactly where the enemy was going to invade, allowing
the king of Israel to avoid surprise attacks. So the king of Syria decided to capture Elisha
and surrounded the town of Dothan, where Elisha was staying, with his army:

*When the servant of the man of God [Elisha] arose early and went out, there
was an army, surrounding the city with horses and chariots. And his servant*

said to him, "Alas, my master! What shall we do?"

So he answered, "Do not fear, for those who are with us are more than those who are with them." And Elisha prayed, and said, "LORD, I pray, open his eyes that he may see." Then the LORD opened the eyes of the young man, and he saw. And behold, the mountain was full of horses and chariots of fire all around Elisha. So when the Syrians came down to him, Elisha prayed to the LORD, and said, "Strike this people, I pray, with blindness." And He struck them with blindness according to the word of Elisha.

Now Elisha said to them, "This is not the way, nor is this the city. Follow me, and I will bring you to the man whom you seek." But he led them to Samaria.

So it was, when they had come to Samaria, that Elisha said, "LORD, open the eyes of these men, that they may see." And the LORD opened their eyes, and they saw; and there they were, inside Samaria!

2 KINGS 6:15–20 NKJV

Elisha did not fear his enemies because he walked by faith—not by sight! He knew God would protect him, that when—not *if*—he prayed, God would send His forces. "The chariots of God are twenty thousand, even thousands of thousands" (Psalm 68:17 NKJV)! Would that we would also see our worldly woes with spiritual vision, that we would open our eyes to the invisible powers of God that come to our rescue! Such "eyesight" would allow us to sit calmly within our physical houses with no fear, knowing that the intangible force of God would allow us to rise above our juggernauts in God's chariots, "in heavenly places in Christ Jesus" (Ephesians 2:6 KJV) where victory over everything below would be ours!

But the story continues. When the king of Israel saw the Syrian forces inside Samaria, he asked Elisha if he should kill them. But Elisha said, "You shall not kill them. . . . Set food and water before them, that they may eat and drink and go to their master" (2 Kings 6:22 NKJV). So a great meal was prepared, and after the soldiers had sated themselves, they were sent back home. "So the bands of Syrian raiders came no more into the land of Israel" (2 Kings 6:23 NKJV).

Elisha's faith and fearlessness allowed him not only to rise above his visible enemies but to do good to them after defeating them (see Proverbs 25:21–22). The result? They stayed away!

Like Elisha, we have a choice. We can allow our juggernauts—big or little—to crush us, plunging us down into fear, defeat, and despair, or we can jump into the chariots of God and rise above them in triumph. All the losses, trials, minor irritations, worries, and woes that come to us become chariots the moment we treat them as such. Smith wrote:

> *Whenever we mount into God's chariots the same thing happens to us spiritually that happened to Elijah. We shall have a translation. Not into the heavens above us, as Elijah did, but into the heaven within us; and this, after all, is almost a grander translation than his. We shall be carried away from the low, earthly groveling plane of life, where everything hurts and everything is unhappy, up into the "heavenly places in Christ Jesus" [Ephesians 2:6], where we can ride in triumph over all below.*

So what steps can we take when, like Elisha's servant, we cry out, "Alas, my master! What shall we do?" (2 Kings 6:15 NKJV), when we have conflicts without and fears within (see 2 Corinthians 7:5). First, we need to quiet ourselves by word and then by vision. We need to find encouragement in God's Word. "Do not fear, for those who are with us are more than those who are with them" (2 Kings 6:16 NKJV). No matter what comes against us—to destroy, offend, or frighten us— God is infinitely more powerful. When we are magnifying the causes of our fear, we need to take hold of ourselves with clear, direct, great, inspiring thoughts of God and His invisible, intangible world. "We know that in all things God works for the good of those who love him. He appointed them to be saved in keeping with his purpose. . . . Since God is on our side, who can be against us?" (Romans 8:28, 31 NIrV). We also know that "God is our place of safety. He gives us strength. He is always there to help us in times of trouble" (Psalm 46:1 NIrV).

Then we must quiet ourselves by vision. Elisha knew by faith that he was safe from the Syrian forces. But he knew his servant was very troubled. So he prayed for him. "LORD, I pray, open his eyes that he may see" (2 Kings 6:17 NKJV). And so the Lord did. The servant's eyes of faith were opened to God's multitude of chariots! This is the prayer we must pray, that God would open our spiritual eyes. Once He does, the dangers of earth and the fear that arises from them will vanish as the darkness before us, allowing us to be carried into the heavenly places in our chariots "paved with love" (Song of Solomon 3:10 KJV). In the temporal world, our chariots won't seem like they are paved with love. Instead they often appear very unattractive. Slights from people we once considered friends. Betrayals by loved ones. The cruelties of neglect, greed, malice, and selfishness practiced in the world. Yet every chariot sent by God (whether of first or second cause) must be paved with love, for our "God is love" (1 John 4:8 KJV).

God is a heavenly rider! Habakkuk tells us that at the Red Sea, He "rode [before] upon Your horses and Your chariots of victory and deliverance" (3:8 AMP). He "rides upon the highest heavens" (Psalm 68:33 NASB). "He makes the clouds His chariot; He walks upon the wings of the wind" (Psalm 104:3 NASB). In His majesty, He rides "prosperously because of truth and meekness and righteousness" (Psalm 45:4 KJV). Thus we must look to God and His chariots to carry us over the trials and tribulations, torments and troubles of this tangible world.

We will not prosper if we look to an earthly conveyance to help us through. For God has told us, "Woe to them that go down to Egypt for help; and stay on horses, and trust in chariots" (Isaiah 31:1 KJV). Our "Egypt" consists of tangible resources we can see. We find ourselves tempted to rely on them because they look real and dependable, whereas God's chariots are intangible and invisible, not seen except by faith. Going "down to Egypt for help" may be depending on money alone to make us feel secure or on certain possessions to make us happy. It may be the counsel of a friend whom we've come to lean on more than God. It may be the Sunday school class or a favorite preacher we believe we can't live without or we will weaken, then die, for lack of spiritual strength.

Anything we rely on other than God will, at some point, be taken away. Smith wrote, "God is obliged often to destroy all our own earthly chariots before He can bring us to the point of mounting into His." He longs to have us depend on Him more than anything or anyone else. For He was, is, and will be the only One we can truly depend on. History proves it. "In the wilderness. . .you saw how the LORD your God carried you, as a father carries his son, all the way you went until you reached this place" (Deuteronomy 1:31 TNIV).

Joseph had a vision of his future victories and reign, but the chariots that took him there—being betrayed by his brothers, sold as a slave, then imprisoned—looked more like juggernauts of agony and failure. Yet because God and His chariots were with him, giving him strength and courage, he did not get discouraged but rose above his earthly cares, even while in a dungeon. Joseph's earthly travails were a strange route to becoming a ruler of Egypt and saving himself and his family, but he could not have gotten there any other way. In the same regard, our road to the heavenly mansion that awaits us is often reached by similar chariots.

Do not allow the juggernauts of this world to roll over you and sink you into the pits of despair, desperation, and fear. Instead, mount up with God, taking each offense, bitter word, tragedy, loss, trial, and temptation as your chariot of God that will take you to the "heavenly places in Christ Jesus" (Ephesians 2:6 KJV). Take the inroad and forget every external obstacle, knowing that God has established your steps (see Psalm 40:2). In doing so, you cannot help but triumph. Become like Paul, whose "thorn in the flesh" and losses were nothing compared to the richness he found in gaining Christ (see Philippians 3:7–9). Instead of allowing worldly woes to cast him down, Paul "[ascribed] strength to God," whose "strength is in the clouds" (Psalm 68:34 NKJV).

Before you may have been blind, but now like Elisha's servant, you see the mighty chariots of God. Take each juggernaut event in your life—big or little—and gird yourself in the Word, open your spiritual eyes, and board the chariot for your soul. Allow your chariot to take you to the heavenly places where you can "ride prosperously" (Psalm 45:4 NKJV) with God on top of all, allowing you to triumph within and without!

There can be no trials in which God's will has not a
place somewhere; and the soul has only to mount into
His will as in a chariot, and it will find itself "riding upon the
heavens" with God in a way it had never dreamed could be.
HANNAH WHITALL SMITH

$\mathcal{P}$ATH MARKERS

$\mathcal{P}$romise

The chariots of God are twenty thousand, even thousands of thousands. . . . Blessed be the Lord, who daily loads us with benefits, the God of our salvation! . . . His strength is in the clouds. O God, You are more awesome than Your holy places. The God of Israel is He who gives strength and power to His people.

PSALM 68:17, 19, 34–35 NKJV

$\mathcal{P}$roof

Therefore, since we have this ministry, as we have received mercy, we do not lose heart. . . . Since we have the same spirit of faith, according to what is written, "I believed and therefore I spoke," we also believe and therefore speak, knowing that He who raised up the Lord Jesus will also raise us up with Jesus, and will present us with you. For all things are for your sakes, that grace, having spread through the many, may cause thanksgiving to abound to the glory of God. Therefore we do not lose heart. Even though our outward man is perishing, yet the inward man is being renewed day by day. For our light affliction, which is but for a moment, is working for us a far more exceeding and eternal weight of glory, while we do not look at the things which are seen, but at the things which are not seen. For the things which are seen are temporary, but the things which are not seen are eternal. . . .

I know a man in Christ who fourteen years ago—whether in the body I do not know, or whether out of the body I do not know, God knows—such a one was caught up to the third heaven. And I know such a man—whether in the body or out of the body I do not know, God knows—how he was caught up into Paradise.

2 CORINTHIANS 4:1, 13–18; 12:2–4 NKJV

Provision

All praise to God, the Father of our Lord Jesus Christ, who has blessed us with every spiritual blessing in the heavenly realms because we are united with Christ.

EPHESIANS 1:3 NLT

Portrait

In Christ, I am raised to new life, setting my eyes on the realities of heaven (see Colossians 3:1).

MIND-RENEWING PRAYERS

DAY 1
Craving Strength and Peace

*Since you have been raised to new life with Christ,
set your sights on the realities of heaven,
where Christ sits in the place of honor at God's right hand.*

COLOSSIANS 3:1 NLT

Lord, I thank You for bringing me new life in Christ. I am setting my sights on Your heavenly kingdom. These troubles here on earth will be but a dim memory someday. So instead of wallowing in self-pity or trying to fix situations on my own, I am going to journey inward to Your side, knowing that when I do, You will give me the strength and peace I crave.

DAY 2
Hope for Tomorrow

"In the wilderness. . .you saw how the LORD your God carried you, as a father carries his son, all the way you went until you reached this place."
DEUTERONOMY 1:31 TNIV

Some days I feel as if I am still wandering around in the wilderness. But You have brought me so far, Lord, I never want to go back. You have carried me through so many heartaches—big and little. Thank You for Your loving care. Although I'm not as far as I think I should be, I praise You for bringing me to where I am today and giving me hope for tomorrow.

DAY 3
Spiritual Vision

"Don't be afraid!" Elisha told him. "For there are more on our side than on theirs!" Then Elisha prayed, "O LORD, open his eyes and let him see!" The LORD opened the young man's eyes, and when he looked up, he saw that the hillside around Elisha was filled with horses and chariots of fire.
2 KINGS 6:16–17 NLT

Show me the true reality, Lord. Reveal Your chariot for me so that I can rise above this world. Remove the scales of worldly woes from my eyes. Open my eyes to the fact that You will never leave me defenseless. Give me twenty-twenty spiritual vision. Your army of hosts is always here to lift me up into the heavens. Save me, Lord. Beam me up now!

Day 4
Far above the Fray

O Lord my God, You are very great. . . . He makes the
clouds His chariot. He walks upon the wings of the wind.
PSALM 104:1, 3 NASB

*Y*ou, God, are grander than I can imagine. All of nature heeds Your voice. You
know my troubles, Lord. Today I lift them up to You. I feel hurt, discouraged, and
anxious. But I know that those emotions are not what I should focus on. So, Lord, keep
me from bowing under the weight of my woes. I raise my eyes to heaven. Mount me up
in Your chariot, far above this fray.

Day 5
Whisked Away

I called on the Lord in my distress. I cried to my God for help. He heard my voice
from his temple, and my cry for help reached his ears. . . . He spread apart the
heavens and came down with a dark cloud under his feet. He rode on one of the
angels as he flew, and he soared on the wings of the wind. . . . He reached down
from high above and took hold of me. He pulled me out of the raging water.
He rescued me from my strong enemy.
PSALM 18:6, 9–10, 16–17 GW

*L*ord, hear my cry! Come rescue me. Reach down from above and pull me out of
this trouble. My heart is heavy, Lord. I can hardly move. Rescue me, for I feel as if I am
drowning in a sea of difficulties. I long to rest in You, to hear Your voice, to feel Your
touch. I have eyes of faith, Lord. Reveal Your chariot and whisk me away!

Day 6
Eyes upon God

O our God. . .we have no might to stand against this great company that is
coming against us. We do not know what to do, but our eyes are upon You.
2 Chronicles 20:12 amp

I don't understand this world, Lord. I feel like such a stranger here. I am so grateful
that I have You to cling to. I am not strong enough to fight this latest battle, Lord. Even
if I did, I'm not sure what to do. So I am looking to You, watching for You, waiting for
You to pull me up into the heavens. You are my rock, my refuge, my rest. You are my
heavenly conqueror!

Day 7
Belief Clears the Path

Believe in the Lord your God and you shall be established;
believe and remain steadfast to His prophets and you shall prosper.
2 Chronicles 20:20 amp

I believe! I believe, Lord! Because You are the great I Am, I know that You will
always be with me. I am sticking to You for all my needs. Make my path clear, God. And
when I am down, give me a lift in Your chariot. Resting in You, trusting You, I know
nothing can harm me. All I need to do is believe.

Chapter 20:
The Life on Wings

*Nothing contributes so much to tranquilize the
mind as a steady purpose—a point on
which the soul may fix its intellectual eye.*
MARY SHELLEY

....

God wants us to fix our soul's intellectual eye upon Him: "You will seek Me, inquire for, and require Me [as a vital necessity] and find Me when you search for Me with all your heart" (Jeremiah 29:13 AMP). If fact, we will be blessed with joy and peace—even amid the storms—when we do so (see Jeremiah 17:7). And the way to keep our eyes on Him is to "wait upon the LORD" (Isaiah 40:31 KJV). The Hebrew word for "wait" is *qawa*, which means to bind together by twisting, to expect—look—patiently.

*Those who wait for the Lord [who expect, look for, and hope in Him] shall
change and renew their strength and power; they shall lift their wings and
mount up [close to God] as eagles [mount up to the sun]; they shall run and
not be weary, they shall walk and not faint or become tired.*

ISAIAH 40:31 AMP

We are told in 1 Corinthians 6:17 that "the person who is joined to the Lord is one spirit with him" (NLT). We are partakers of His divine nature (see 2 Peter 1:4). With our soul's eye on Him and our spirit joined with His, we can mount up as eagles to the highest heights, eternally secure and protected, with an open doorway to all of God's blessings (see John 10:28; Romans 8:31–39; Hebrews 7:25; 1 Peter 1:4).

Christ is our high place—in Him we have our foundation. In Him we make our nest, like an eagle in the highest tree or cliff face. As new women hidden in Christ, we are His fledglings.

Yet how do we learn to fly spiritually? The same way an eaglet does.

Oddly enough, eaglets are not born with instinctive knowledge about how to fly or hunt. Shortly after birth, an eaglet will become attached to the first moving object it sees! This is a process called *imprinting*. For the bald eagle, this imprinting period begins at the time it is able to first focus its eyes (approximately nine days old) and ends at about six weeks. If a baby eagle receives food or care from any source other than an adult eagle during this time, it becomes emotionally attached to that provider.

God is our Creator, source, and provider. When we are spiritually reborn, the first thing we "see" is Christ and His life. It is to Him we look and to Him we become attached. We do not instinctively know how to fly spiritually, but we can learn by imitating Christ (see 1 Corinthians 11:1). We'll never get off the ground, however, until we first strengthen our bodies and our wings. We do that by waiting on God as a baby eagle waits upon its parents to feed, protect, and teach it.

As we wait upon the Lord, we are also abiding in Him, hidden in Christ. Resting in Him in that "secret place of the Most High" as Psalm 91:1 (AMP) says, we "remain stable and fixed under the shadow of the Almighty [Whose power no foe can withstand]." And the benefits in that secret place are amazing! In making God our refuge and fortress, we are protected against anything and everything. As we learn to lean and rely upon Him, our confidence and trust build! He will be the first place we run. And there's more! The myriad of amazing promises found in Psalm 91—preservation, help, protection, renewed strength and courage, patience, hope, daily blessings, and more—can be realized only when we have determined to trust and surrender ourselves to our loving God.

As we wait upon Him, we do so prayerfully (see Psalm 25:4–5), seeking His pathway for us and hoping in Him. We wait with patience (see Psalm 37:7; 145:15), not getting overanxious. We learn how to sit still and not fret over every little thing, knowing that He will provide us with the food we need, when we need it. With single-mindedness of purpose, we abide in Him (see Psalm 62:5), putting heart, mind, soul, and strength wholly into the endeavor, and we do it expectantly (see Psalm 62:5–6; 123:2; Micah 7:7), longingly (see Psalm 130:5–6), quietly (see Lamentations 3:26), and continually (see Hosea 12:6). It's an ongoing process that leads not only to joy but to peace!

To increase our strength, we stay deep in His Word and constantly renew our minds—day by day, second by second (see Romans 12:2). We do this by rejecting what the worldlings think and how they feel (see Ephesians 4:17). We renounce their ignorance of God and hardness of heart (see Ephesians 4:18). Instead, we learn about (see Ephesians 4:20) and watch Christ.

As we constantly take hold of our fresh mental and spiritual attitudes, we develop a new nature, the one God planned for in the beginning of time. Having learned Christ, we attain new knowledge (see Colossians 3:10) and thus attain gifts from God (see 2 Timothy 1:6–7). He bestows upon us a spirit of boldness (see Romans 8:15). We have the courage to leave our comfort zones. He bestows a spirit of power (see Luke 24:49; Acts 1:8; 1 Corinthians 16:10; 1 Timothy 4:14) to soar upon the heavens, take new challenges, and serve Him. He gives us a spirit of love (see 1 Corinthians 13:4) for our friends, enemies, and God Himself, prompting us to encourage and forgive others and to pant after Him. Finally, He gives us the spirit of a sound mind, which gives us understanding, peace, and self-control (see Galatians 5:22–23).

We have been well fed as God, our eagle parent, has brought us the food of His Word, giving us new insights each time we look to Him for answers (see Psalm 63:7). Now we have grown to the point of soon being able to really try out our wings—one of which is trust and the other surrender. For if we have only one wing—trust or surrender—we never rise above the nest. We need two wings—trust *and* surrender—to become airborne!

Our eyesight is as sharp as our papa eagle's. Still in our nest but far above the world, we have keener perception and view things more clearly, for we are looking from a God-perspective. Our problems no longer look interminable or insurmountable or significant.

God is teaching us to be like Christ. So our parent eagle now "stirs up its nest" yet still "hovers over its young, spreading out its wings, taking them up, carrying them on its wings" (Deuteronomy 32:11 NKJV). God permits us to have troubles so that we don't get comfortable where we are but leave our nests—our comfort zones. Yet while we are in the midst of our ongoing transformations, as we become more and more like Christ, He continually cares for and protects us as we grow stronger and stronger. And when necessary, He will carry us until we are ready to soar where He wants us to soar.

Tentatively at first, we follow our Master, first rising above our nests in brief test flights. The more we allow our souls to fly up out of ourselves, fueled with His courage and steeped in Christlikeness, we leave our comfort zone and take flight. We become full-fledged eagles!

An eagle knows when a storm is on its way long before it breaks. Able to rise above the earthly tempest and soar into the heavens, it seeks a high spot and waits for the winds to come. Like eagles, we, too, can soar above the storms when we spread our wings and allow the Holy Spirit to lift up our spirits. As full-fledged eagles, we can rise high above the storms of life, taking each and every opportunity to do as Jesus did.

But if we find ourselves weak—emotionally, spiritually, physically, mentally—we know that if we do not have the strength to fly, we can always look to God as our "place of refuge and a shelter from the storm and from rain" (see Isaiah 4:6 AMP). Amid life's tumults and tempests, all we need to do is pray, and God will either cover us or give us the strength we need to soar.

> *Be merciful and gracious to me, O God, be merciful and gracious to me,*
> *for my soul takes refuge and finds shelter and confidence in You; yes, in the*
> *shadow of Your wings will I take refuge and be confident until calamities and*
> *destructive storms are passed.*

PSALM 57:1 AMP

Holocaust survivor Victor Frankl said, "Everything can be taken from man but one thing: the last of human freedoms—to choose one's attitude in any given set of circumstances—to choose one's way." Which way do you choose? The path of happiness by trusting in and surrendering all to the Lord, allowing you to abide in Jesus, wait upon God, and soar above the storms empowered by the Holy Spirit? Or the path of captivity by this world, tethered by ropes of discouragement, disappointment, wrongdoing, doubt, and fear?

We can fly only when we do three things. First is to *use* our wings, for we won't get one inch off the ground unless we do. And why should we walk around or tunnel through our sometimes mountainous obstacles if we can fly above them?

The second thing we must do to fly is not look to our emotions. We cannot depend on them, for often they are false indicators of our spiritual reality. Instead, we rely solely on our wings of entire surrender to God and absolute trust in Him.

And the third thing we must do to fly is to stop looking to earthly solutions to our problems. Like the Israelites, we are not to "flee upon horses" (Isaiah 30:16 KJV), because if we do, we will find that our enemies will have swifter ones and quickly catch up to us. Our best assurance is to look to God, who wants our eyes constantly upon Him (see Isaiah 30:20 AMP) and longs to rescue us from every earthly temptation, sin, sorrow, and trial.

> *The Lord [earnestly] waits [expecting, looking, and longing] to be gracious to you; and therefore He lifts Himself up, that He may have mercy on you and show loving-kindness to you. For the Lord is a God of justice. Blessed (happy, fortunate, to be envied) are all those who [earnestly] wait for Him, who expect and look and long for Him [for His victory, His favor, His love, His peace, His joy, and His matchless, unbroken companionship]!*
>
> ISAIAH 30:18 AMP

We will be more than conquerors (see Romans 8:37) as we "seek those things which are above" and not "things of the earth" because our lives are "hid with Christ in God" (Colossians 3:1–3 KJV). We who "wait upon the LORD. . .shall mount up with wings as eagles" (Isaiah 40:31 KJV)—not "perhaps mount up" but "shall"! So lift up your soul and allow the power of the Holy Spirit to lift you up in flight, knowing that the imprint of Christ is upon you as you pray, feast upon the Word, and wait upon the Lord. Sing a song to the Lord in the midst of your trials, and you will be as Christ, "sorrowful, yet always rejoicing. . .poor, yet making many rich. . .having nothing, and yet possessing all things" (2 Corinthians 6:10 NKJV).

> *God wants you to be an "eagle Christian," one who can fly high, be bold, live with power, keep circumstances and relationships in perspective, live at peace, stay strong, and soar above the storms of life.*
>
> JOYCE MEYER, *NEVER GIVE UP!*

$\mathcal{P}$ATH MARKERS

$\mathcal{P}$romise

Those who wait upon GOD get fresh strength. They spread their wings and soar like eagles, they run and don't get tired, they walk and don't lag behind.

ISAIAH 40:31 MSG

$\mathcal{P}$roof

The LORD found Israel in a desert land. He found them in an empty and windy wasteland. He took care of them and kept them safe. He guarded them as he would guard his own eyes. He was like an eagle that stirs up its nest. It hovers over its little ones. It spreads out its wings to catch them. It carries them on its feathers. The LORD was the only one who led Israel. No other god was with them. The LORD made them ride on the highest places in the land.

DEUTERONOMY 32:10–13 NIrV

$\mathcal{P}$rovision

For He will give His angels charge concerning you, to guard you in all your ways. They will bear you up in their hands, that you do not strike your foot against a stone.

PSALM 91:11–12 NASB

$\mathcal{P}$ortrait

In Christ, I am raised up and sitting in heaven (see Ephesians 2:6).

Mind-Renewing Prayers

Day 1
In the Secret Place

He who dwells in the secret place of the Most High shall abide under
the shadow of the Almighty. I will say of the Lord, "He is my refuge
and my fortress; my God, in Him I will trust."
Psalm 91:1–2 NKJV

Lord, my eyes are looking up to You. I long to live in Your presence, in the secret place, hidden in Christ. Here with You, I am no longer afraid. I know that when I am with You, nothing and no one can hurt me. You are an amazing fortress, impenetrable. Bless my soul, Lord. I trust in You to keep me safe within Your arms and to strengthen me in Your love and light.

Day 2
A Winged Refuge

Surely He shall deliver you from the snare of the fowler and from the perilous
pestilence. He shall cover you with His feathers, and under His wings you shall
take refuge; His truth shall be your shield and buckler. You shall not be afraid.
Psalm 91:3–5 NKJV

I'm ducking for cover in You, Lord. Keep me safe from these worldly things that are begging for my attention. I rise up to You; hide me under Your wings. Keep my feet free from snares. Help me understand that You will never leave me nor forsake me, that I can abide with You not only when I am afraid but every moment of every day, looking to You for wisdom and strength.

Day 3
Forces to Be Reckoned With

Praise the LORD, you angels, you mighty ones who carry out his plans,
listening for each of his commands. Yes, praise the LORD,
you armies of angels who serve him and do his will!
PSALM 103:20–21 NLT

God, thank You for sending reinforcements to watch over me. Although they are invisible, I know Your angels are forces to be reckoned with. So I will not be afraid, no matter what comes into my life. For with Your presence, the Holy Spirit's power, and Christ's love, I won't trip and fall headlong into trouble. You will keep me safe.

Day 4
Free Flying

"Because he has set his love upon Me, therefore I will deliver him;
I will set him on high, because he has known My name. He shall call upon Me,
and I will answer him; I will be with him in trouble; I will deliver him and
honor him. With long life I will satisfy him, and show him My salvation."
PSALM 91:14–16 NKJV

I love You, Lord, with all my heart, mind, body, and soul. Lift me up into Your presence. Let me see things from a higher perspective, for I feel overwhelmed. Deliver me from the ties that bind me. I want my spirit to fly freely with You, up above this world and all its woes. For the true light, the true life, the true love is all tied up in You, and it is there I want to be.

DAY 5
Peace and Quiet

This is what the Almighty LORD, the Holy One of Israel, says:
You can be saved by returning to me. You can have rest.
You can be strong by being quiet and by trusting me.
ISAIAH 30:15 GW

*S*omehow, Lord, I feel as if I have fallen out of my nest, my foundation in Christ. My wings are tired, Lord, and I don't want to spiral down. So let me stay with You for a while, resting until I can soar again. In You, I am saved from the calamities that rush at me. Build up my strength, Lord, as I linger here with You, in peace and quiet, in love and trust.

DAY 6
Lifted Spirit

For He commands and raises the stormy wind, which lifts up the
waves of the sea. . . . He calms the storm, so that its waves are still.
PSALM 107:25, 29 NKJV

*G*od, at Your call the earth shakes, the mountains rumble, the lightning strikes, the rains come, the sea rises, and the storm rages. Right now, Lord, I feel so out of control, so weak. But I know I am not to live according to my emotions. So please, Lord, calm the tempest within me and without. Give me peace in Your presence. Lift my spirit to bind with Yours.

Day 7
Lifted Eyes

*And He raised us up together with Him and made us sit down
together [giving us joint seating with Him] in the heavenly sphere
[by virtue of our being] in Christ Jesus (the Messiah, the Anointed One).*
EPHESIANS 2:6 AMP

Jesus, I come to You, my burdens falling off my back as I lift my eyes to the
heavens. My spirit longs to feel Your presence, to see Your face, to touch the hem of Your
robe. Because of Your love for me, I can rest here in You. You give me the power to live
this life for You. Teach me Your way. Guide me. Whisper in my ear. Fly with me to the
Father of lights.

Conclusion:
The Pathway to Happiness

*God created you in His own image, and He wants you
to experience His joy and abundance. But God will not
force His joy upon you; you must claim it.*
BETH MOORE, *PRAYERS AND PROMISES FOR WOMEN*

....

It has been said that sometimes God writes straight with crooked lines. . . .

In the late 1950s, a high school teacher named Harry Hanners was struck with tuberculosis of the spine. He underwent several operations, spent months in traction, and had to learn to walk again. For the pain, he was given a prescription derived from morphine, to which he eventually became addicted. His wife, who happened to be a registered nurse, perceived his addiction and begged him to take a leave of absence from work and enter a clinic to help him break the habit. She knew that although the drugs did not cloud his mind, allowing him to return to teaching and pursue a master's degree, they would eventually wreak havoc on his nervous system. Harry, knowing they were too much in debt for him to stop working again, refused.

After Harry's physician declined to write any more prescriptions for Harry, the schoolteacher began to obtain the drugs illegally. He went to various doctors for new prescriptions then filled them at different pharmacies.

The longer Harry stayed on the painkillers, the stronger his habit grew and the more he lashed out at his wife and children. Finally, his wife threatened to take the children and leave him if Harry didn't get off the pills. He agreed, and after three months he gained victory over his addiction. Just when the couple thought they were in the clear, Harry was arrested outside the high school where he taught and had just been promoted. Charged with fraudulently procuring narcotics, Harry refused his wife's plea to hire a lawyer. Instead, he pled guilty, knowing that doing so would mean the end of his teaching job.

Devastated at this turn of events, Harry's wife visited her pastor. Through tears, she said, "When I think of all the prayers and all the tortuous hours of agony. . . He promised to cure himself and he did. He cured himself and now this. It's just so unjust. Why doesn't God help us? Why doesn't God help us?"

Her minister replied, "He will. He will. How many times have I told you: God writes straight with crooked lines."

"But I—"

"What you've got to do is pray for patience and trust."

Days later, Harry's wife went to visit her husband in prison and found out he'd been teaching some of the other prisoners, mostly teenagers and addicts who had never finished school. He'd started thinking, *There are lots of students, and I'm a teacher. . .*

His wife asked, "You're teaching school here?"

Harry replied, "Why not? It keeps them busy, keeps my mind off myself. We got permission from the warden."

His wife responded, "Oh Harry, I'm so proud of you."

Months later, Harry was released from prison and met with the warden. One of the boys Harry had taught, previously considered incorrigible, had gotten out and begun his own business. So the warden offered Harry a job teaching in the county jail—the only school of its kind.

Harry said, "A job. . .teaching. . .where it will do the most good and it's needed the most." Having been told his pay wouldn't be very much at first, but if he was patient, it would work itself out, Harry accepted the job offer.

His wife, with a far-off look in her eyes, said softly, "Patience. . . God *does* write straight with crooked lines."

Our pathways to happiness in the Lord are often straight with crooked lines. The important thing for us is to remain patient and trusting as we wait on the Lord. Continue to surrender yourself to Him and know that although He may be taking you the long way around, you *will* become the woman He has created you to be.

God never shuts a door without opening another. So do not be discouraged if you are not yet the woman you'd like to be or if you are not doing what you think God has meant you to do. Just be patient, surrender, trust, and know that your loving God is doing everything for your good.

And while you are traveling down the pathway of happiness, following Christ as you walk in the Way, daily remind yourself who you are in Christ. Write your portrait attributes upon your heart so that when feelings of dismay, fear, or discouragement threaten to overwhelm you and thoughts from the dark side begin careening around in your head, you may call up these truths, calm yourself, and bring in the light.

For your convenience, your portrait's "features" are listed on page 246. And if in your journey, you find other attributes you'd like to add to this "sketch," please do so!

Each day, "put on the new self, which is being renewed in knowledge in the image of its Creator" (Colossians 3:10 TNIV), and allow your happiness in the Lord, which is strong and eternal, to overrule happenings. "Always be full of joy in the Lord. I say it again—rejoice!" (Philippians 4:4 NLT). And trust in the process: "If it seems slow in coming, wait patiently, for it will surely take place. It will not be delayed" (Habakkuk 2:3 NLT).

The Lord bless you and watch, guard, and keep you;
the Lord make His face to shine upon and enlighten you
and be gracious (kind, merciful, and giving favor) to you;
the Lord lift up His [approving] countenance upon you
and give you peace (tranquility of heart and life continually).
NUMBERS 6:24–26 AMP

Portrait

In Christ. . .

I am able to have joy in any situation (see Philippians 4:4, 12).

I am being transformed into a new person (see 2 Corinthians 5:17).

I know God will provide me with everything I need (see Philippians 4:19).

I am standing firm (see 1 Thessalonians 3:8).

I am holy, pure in God's sight, and empowered by the Holy Spirit (see Ephesians 1:4).

I live by faith, not sight (see 2 Corinthians 5:7).

I have access to God's will (see 1 John 5:14).

I have access to God's wisdom and direction (see 1 Corinthians 1:30).

I have inherited God's promises (see 2 Peter 1:3–4).

I am more than a conqueror (see Romans 8:37).

I am not only redeemed but forgiven (see Ephesians 1:7).

I am assured of God's presence in any and all situations (see Isaiah 43:2).

I am a free woman, a daughter of God, and an heir of His promises (see Galatians 4:7).

I am growing in the grace and knowledge of the Lord (see 2 Peter 3:18).

I am strong enough to do whatever God calls me to do (see Philippians 4:13).

I am spiritually transformed with energy, strength, and purpose every day (see Romans 12:1–2).

I am loved by God and delight to do His will (see John 14:21).

I am spiritually blessed because He lives in me (see Ephesians 1:3).

I am raised to new life, setting my eyes on the realities of heaven (see Colossians 3:1).

I am raised up and sitting in heaven (see Ephesians 2:6).

"Now I'm turning you over to God, our marvelous God whose gracious Word can make you into what he wants you to be and give you everything you could possibly need in this community of holy friends."
ACTS 20:32 MSG

Notes

Notes

1. W. P. Livingstone, *Mary Slessor of Calabar* (University of Michigan Library, 1917).
2. http://curiosity.discovery.com/question/what-age-body-stops-growing.
3. Ibid.
4. Wikipedia defines a juggernaut "in colloquial English usage. . .[as] a literal or metaphorical force regarded as mercilessly destructive and unstoppable. Originating ca. 1850, the term is a metaphorical reference to the Hindu Ratha Yatra temple car, which apocryphally was reputed to crush devotees under its wheels." *Merriam-Webster's Collegiate Dictionary,* 11th ed., defines *juggernaut* as "a large heavy truck" or "a massive inexorable force, campaign, movement, or object that crushes whatever is in its path."

About the Author

Donna K. Maltese is a freelance writer, an editor, and a coach, as well as a publicist for a local Mennonite project. Residing in Bucks County, Pennsylvania, with her husband and two adult children, Donna is active in her local church and enjoys serving with Mennonite Disaster Service.

Scripture Index